GETTING WET

GETTING WET

ADVENTURES
IN THE
JAPANESE BATH

Eric Talmadge

KODANSHA INTERNATIONAL
Tokyo • New York • London

Distributed in the United States by Kodansha America Inc., and in the United Kingdom and continental Europe by Kodansha Europe Ltd.

Published by Kodansha International Ltd., 17–14 Otowa 1-chome, Bunkyo-ku, Tokyo 112–8652, and Kodansha America, Inc.

First edition, 2006
15 14 13 12 11 10 09 08 07 06   10 9 8 7 6 5 4 3 2 1

Library of Congress Cataloging-in-Publication Data

Talmadge, Eric.
  Getting wet : adventures in the Japanese bath / by Eric Talmadge. -- 1st ed.
      p. cm.
   Includes index.
   ISBN-13: 978–4–7700–3020–7
   ISBN-10: 4–7700–3020–7
  1. Bathing customs--Japan. 2. Prostitution--Japan. I. Title.
GT2846.J3T35 2006
391.6'4--dc22

                                        2006010111

www.kodansha-intl.com

CONTENTS

ONE TOE AT A TIME

THE ODD REALIZATION that I have lived in Japan longer than in my native country hit me one night a few years ago while I was in the tub.

I was nineteen when I climbed into my blue Volvo and for the last time pulled out of my family's rhododendron-lined driveway in Olympia, Washington, a tidy little emerald of a Pacific coast town. It was only an hour-long drive up the I-5 freeway to Sea-Tac Airport, south of Seattle. But that drive in the summer of 1981 turned out to be the beginning of a very long, one-way trip.

After I had made the decision to go, I reveled in the novelty of leaving the town behind to go to college not just in the Big City, but, arguably, in the Biggest City. And a foreign one—a really foreign one—at that. It would be a great adventure. For a small-town boy, it offered some terrific bragging rights. Friends were impressed. Parties were thrown. My parents were proud. I was even interviewed by the local newspaper.

Though the reporter who came out to talk to me seemed to think I was terribly brave, and probably more than a little weird, it was a calculatedly tame thing to do. I'd been to Japan before, for nearly a year in high school, and I knew that it was a safe, clean, and easy place to get along.

Okay, I know, it's a cliché. But the Japanese really are a very well-organized people. Things are done properly here. Trains run more or less on time. The water doesn't make you sick. America is an ally. Attempts at learning the language and customs are appreciated, almost overly so. The department of Comparative Cultures at Sophia University, where I was to spend the next three years, was run by Catholics and full of foreigners like myself. Better yet, even the limited Japanese I had picked up during my high school stint gave me a head-start over the total newbies, who looked up to me as a guy who could get around on his own.

There is a point, however, when the law of diminishing returns kicks in. One never becomes Japanese. And while I've always been comfortable with that—turning Japanese has never been my goal—it is not always easy being a permanent *gaijin*, or foreigner.

Before too long, the point of celebrating the passing of another year began to fade. Five, ten, twenty years . . . after one hits a certain tenure, it's all the same. Now utterly unable to locate me in their frame of reference, the annual flock of newbies who once found me useful and impressive now look on me as an expatriate lifer, a concept that, like running off to join the circus, smacks of extremism and, because there is no return home, seems to defeat the whole purpose of going abroad to begin with. The Japanese— some quite openly, though most keep it to themselves—tend to consider the long-timer as an oddball who should have left long, long ago.

So, if you're smart, you just carve out your little niche, and go about your life. It's like birthdays as you get older. They come, they go. With or without a cake. So at forty, I quietly, without blowing out any candles, turned the more-out-than-in corner.

I SUPPOSE IT'S NOT surprising I realized that in the bath.

The Japanese spend a lot of time in the bath, and the way the bath is set up, it is a very conducive place for reflection. Instead of taking a shower in the morning, the more common routine is to bathe sometime after eating dinner and before going to bed. Not long after I first came to Japan in 1976, my host family actually bought a newfangled water heater so I could take a quick, hot shower in the morning. Until then, they had just heated the water slowly at night like everybody else in their rural, rice paddy-ringed community. But until the day I left, I continued to be the only one to ever take morning showers in their home. Though it was a kind gesture on their behalf, I always felt they looked on the whole idea as a tremendously silly, and culturally inferior, Americanism.

Things have changed since then. Young people, especially single young women, have adopted the morning shower in greater numbers. In the cities, it has become a pretty well established norm, as is evidenced by the common sight of wet-haired "office ladies" rushing to the commuter trains each morning. It even has its own Japlish name: *asa-shan*, a combination of the Japanese word for morning, and the first syllable of the transliterated English word "shampoo."

Even so, the nightly bath remains a common household tradition in Japan, and having accepted the urban Japanese way of life as my own a long time ago, much of the self-reflection I have done in my adult life I have done, like most Japanese adults, in a tub of hot water.

While I have always been fond of the Japanese style of bathing, it took me much longer to succumb to their penchant for hot springs. I'd been to a few in college with my friends, and the trips were great fun. After that, every few years I would end up in one for some reason or another, which is par for the course. The spas are everywhere. Like karaoke bars or sushi joints, it's hard not to stumble into one at some point. But hot springs, like sushi joints and karaoke bars, are something I never sought out on my own.

That changed with the Nagano Olympics. As the senior correspondent for The Associated Press in Tokyo in 1998, I was assigned to scope out Nagano ahead of the Games. I was the AP's advance guy, the local expert, and it was my job to check out the venues, write about what kind of a place Nagano was, and then live there for more than a month, covering the event start to finish.

It was one of the most enjoyable assignments of my career. And it took me to the heart of hot spring country. I was able to soak up the waters of Nozawa Onsen, a beautiful old spa and ski resort that was to be the cross-country and biathlon venue. For a color piece, I made the pilgrimage to the nine baths of Shibu Onsen, just down the hill from the Olympic half-pipe and snowboarding courses. And for a longish scene-setter, I hiked through the woods of Jigokudani and joined Nagano's famous snow monkeys for a dip in what turned out to be an almost unbearably hot pool of volcanically heated mineral water.

Early on in the Games, I had become friends with my AP colleagues from London and Brussels, and a trio of journalists from the next Winter Olympic venue, Salt Lake City. I don't now remember whose idea it was, but one slow news day we decided that, before the Games ended and we all went our separate ways, we had to go see the snow monkeys.

It was an easy trip, involving only a couple of short train and bus rides and then a half-hour hike there and back. By this time, I had been to that neck of the woods often enough to have a favorite inn along the way. So, before getting on the bus back to Nagano City, I stopped by to say hello.

Though we were a group of eight (a young couple from California had joined us on the trail), the owner insisted we couldn't leave without having a soak. We hadn't bathed at the hot springs where the monkeys reside, so we appreciated the offer.

As is common in older spas, this one had three bathing areas, one for men, one for women, and a mixed zone between the two. Our group was evenly divided and after washing off in our respective gender-specific areas, we meandered into the outdoor mixed zone for what turned out to be probably the closest thing I have had yet to the ideal hot springs experience—a controlled mental meltdown, when all the normal flotsam of the brain recedes, allowing the warmth of the moment and the beauty of nature to seep slowly into one's core.

When we came out of the bath, the innkeeper had a room waiting for us. There was a stick of incense burning in the alcove. Green tea and apple slices cut to resemble rabbits were set out for each person in the group. Everything was on the house. Just remember Nagano fondly, the innkeeper said.

I always have.

THIS BOOK IS NOT an attempt to find the best bath in the whole country, or the ultimate hot springs inn. I hope instead to offer a glimpse into what Japan's bathing scene is all about, since for many it is, in fact, more "cult" than "culture."

That discovery gave me a whole new way of looking at the nation I have called home for so long.

And, of course, I have the bath itself to thank for the epiphany.

Yokohama, 2006

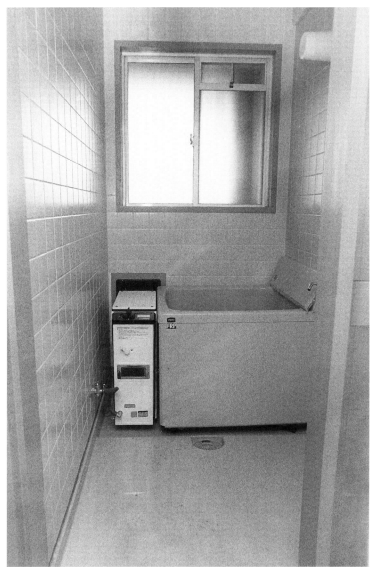

『伊香保の街』　……　与謝野晶子

榛名山の一角に、段また段を成して

羅馬時代の野外劇場の如く

あに刻み附けられた　梯敷形の伊香保の街、

屋根の上に屋根　　雛屋の上に部屋

すべてが温泉宿である、そして椿の若葉の光が

柔かい緑で　　　　街全體を濡して為る

I

GETTING WET

*Reflections on the Japanese love of soaking,
from a visit to a hot springs to active volcanoes
and the customs of the home bath*

I AM STARK NAKED, immersed up to my chin in an outdoor pool of smelly, near-scalding water with a half-dozen equally exposed, wrinkly old men.

I am here of my own volition. In fact, I paid to get in.

And I'm kind of enjoying myself.

A couple of the men are in the middle of a hushed chat, but the others are silent, their eyes closed lightly as rivulets of sweat roll down their foreheads and cheeks. There is a cool breeze wafting through a rickety bamboo partition that obscures the view of the one-lane mountain road just a few meters away and separates the male and female sections of the bath. A lonely *hototogisu*, a drab-looking songbird that is nonetheless much prized by Japanese poets, chirps energetically in the tall, crooked pine trees that shelter us from the late-morning sun. There is a strong aroma of the woods, the damp soil and tree bark, in the air.

Every now and then, the chirping of the bird mixes with bursts of laughter from the women on the other side of the divide. I imagine that, like the men around me, they are in their sixties or seventies. They must be tourists, probably overnighters. Judging from their accents, they are most likely from the city of Nagoya, a half-day bus trip away.

Kenzo Tamura—the bath's manager, an affable, athletic man in his forties with a buzz cut and a bright-blue aloha shirt—warned me before I got in that there was a bit of a crowd. Often, he said, at this time of day, at this time of year, the bath would be completely empty.

For a city dweller like me, his apology turns out to be almost ironic. In some public baths in Tokyo, getting splashed by the next-bather-over's used soap water—or even getting elbowed—is part of the package. Here I have all the space I need.

Quickly, I am absorbed into my own little private world of wet heat. The pungent, rust-tinted water feels smooth, almost slippery, and soft—telltale signs of the minerals within. Each ripple created by even the slightest shifting of my fellow bathers brings a renewed rush of heat, and each breeze brings an intensely pleasant coolness.

The water is taking over. The bath is a cocktail, and I am its maraschino cherry. It's been only about ten minutes, but already my head is beginning to empty and my innards feel as though they are starting to liquefy. In a good way.

As I languish against a submerged crag, I can almost hear the blood coursing up from my organs and racing to the vascular hinterlands of the outer layers of my skin, in a panicked effort to keep me cool. My face is flushed, my pores are all the way open. My arms and legs feel heavy. And light at the same time. I'm floating away.

But I stay in for a few more minutes. Like everyone else, I have a little hand towel, and I use it to wipe my forehead. It is wet and refreshingly cool.

The bath, with its figure-eight shape, isn't very big. It reminds me of a backyard pool, the kind a few of my friends had in American suburbia. The water is less than three feet deep in most places. Its steam rises in a slow swirl and then dissipates over the rocks set around the bath to create the ambiance of a Zen garden. At one end, a steady gush drops like a miniature waterfall from an unadorned gray plastic pipe. Its sound, and the banter of the few bathers who talk, provides a sort of calming white noise.

When I rise from the water, my head spins.

I now have my own personal waterline. From the neck down, I am red as a well-boiled lobster. I'm naked to the world, one with the great outdoors. I'm feeling fine, almost like I have an afterglow. I might even like to strut about a bit, do some push-ups or something, if the water hadn't turned my joints to Jell-O.

But it's time to put my clothes back on and get to work.

A FLIGHT OF three hundred and sixty uneven stone steps starts at the foot of the tilted mountain village of Ikaho and winds upward to its heart, a gushing well of steaming-hot, brownish-red spring water. Set back at the end of a narrow road behind a weathered Shinto shrine, the fountainhead is protected by a dome of thick plastic. Bronze plaques and a statue nearby denote how this spot came to be at the center of what is now one of Japan's greatest passions.

Somewhere between five hundred and one thousand years ago, depending on which local history you believe, a curious local nobleman discovered that not only did a seemingly endless flow of hot water keep gushing out of the mountainside, but the water, despite being a bit metallic, was good to drink and relaxing to soak in.

The progression from there was probably inevitable. At first, with travel arduous and permits hard to come by, the natural springs were used mainly by samurai, the Buddhist priesthood, and local villagers. But by the seventeenth century, Ikaho was drawing health-seekers of every social stripe and from increasingly distant towns. Even the privileged classes from the swelling capital of Edo were beginning to work their way northward into the range of mountains capped by Haruna, a long-dormant volcano where this tiny, quiet village is located.

By the 1800s, the town's metamorphosis into a tourist trap was complete. "Until recently, Ikaho was but little known, and frequently only by the holiday folk of the neighboring region," Henry Spencer Palmer wrote in an article in *The Times of London* in August 1886. "This—a mere handful of a place, yet capable at a pinch of accommodating between two thousand to three thousand guests in its short summer season—is Ikaho, now fast becoming one of the most popular spas in Japan."

The scenery along the stone steps that make up the self-consciously quaint main street (cars must snake their way through a series of back alleys) is pretty much the same as it was when Palmer—among the first wave of foreigners allowed to wander Japan after the country was reopened to the world in 1868—described its charms. Lined with small inns, eateries, sake bars, and souvenir shops, it retains the look of a Japan that long ago vanished from the larger cities. The smell of a ubiquitous snack called *takoyaki*—batter-covered octopus chunks topped off with seaweed—mixes in the crisp highland air with that of green tea ice cream.

But Ikaho is no longer bringing in tourists by the thousands. Not by a long shot. In a typical year, five *million* bathers will soak in its waters. A fantastically complex system of overground pipes—some still made of bamboo—delivers the spring water, still hot, from the main well to dozens of thirsty public and private bathhouses, inns, and fancy new hotels, without which the village would shrivel up and die.

Success, however, has muddied the waters.

When I took my first plunge into the waters of Ikaho in the late summer of 2004, the whole town was embroiled in one of the most shocking scandals not involving politicians or sex to engulf Japan in years. The nation's hot springs industry had been caught resorting to all kinds of dirty tricks to fill ever-larger baths and accommodate the ever-growing crowds.

Venerable spas were caught topping off their tubs with tap or regular well-water; others were using a cocktail of chemical coloring agents to add the desired milky color to mineral water that had been spread too thin and lost its natural oomph. Police raided some of the country's most famous hot spring resorts, Ikaho included. A handful of inns were forced to shut down. The government's Environmental Agency began a much-publicized review of the notoriously porous regulations defining what can and cannot be advertised as a hot spring, and travel agencies were thanking their lucky stars that the news broke during the off-season. Hot springs are, after all, by far the country's most lucrative domestic tourist attraction.

The revelations, though, came as no surprise to industry insiders. Tampering with the water had long been an established, though not much talked about, practice at resorts. The government had even issued a scathing, though little-noticed, report years before that suggested widespread chicanery.

But when the scandal was splashed across the pages of a popular weekly magazine, bringing the story to the bathing masses, it hit like a tsunami. It was on and off the front pages for months. I wrote it up for a story that went out to newspapers around the world. The *New York Times* and *Washington Post* soon had similar pieces of their own.

The reason was clear. Though of little real practical significance—a deadly outbreak of Legionnaire's disease two years before created less of a stir—the allegations struck at the very heart of one of Japan's dearest beliefs: the sanctity of the bath.

"People don't come here just to get clean," Tamura told me as I had a cup of coffee on a wooden bench outside his bath, which is just a stone's throw from the Ikaho fountainhead. "They come here to cleanse their souls."

WELL BEFORE THE Romans were establishing themselves at Bath, the Japanese were absorbing the natural heat percolating up from underneath their feet.

In a great confluence of a people and their land, Japan is both a population of relentless energy and a landscape of geological restlessness. Alternately crushed and torn by the incessant movement of the great jigsaw puzzle pieces that make up the crust of Earth, the land is never at ease. It sits atop three tectonic plates—one of which cuts right through its main island—and is close to the boundaries of yet another. There are dozens of active volcanoes here, several in a state of constant eruption. Even the sublime Mount Fuji, with its gentle slopes and near-perfect symmetry, is alive and well, steaming and bulging and threatening in the not-too-distant future to send its columns of steam and gas into the sky and its gray ash raining down—yet again—on Tokyo.

Offshore, just beyond the beaches where the nation summers, underwater volcanoes spit up their roiling guts, sending yellow streams of sulfur and gas off to sea. Farther out, the craters of bigger, more established volcanoes poke out from the Pacific, periodically erupting with such violence that whole islands must be evacuated. Though shows of slow-moving lava, à la Hawaiian volcanoes, are rare, Japan's can be even more deadly. Eruptions climax in pyroclastic flows, a bubbling mixture of super-heated gas, ash, and other ejecta that races down a volcano's side at speeds much too fast for even a car to outrun, suffocating, frying, and burying its victims.

The less spectacular variety just belches invisible gas, though these volcanoes are even more insidious. Often, the gas, though odorless, is highly noxious and prone to linger in valleys and depressions as if in wait for unknowing villagers to return.

Hazard maps showing fault lines make the country look more like a geologist's worst-case scenario than an incredibly pricey piece of real estate. Nuclear reactors are built near faults. Tokyo's emergency center, where tons of supplies for the next big seismic disaster are stored, is right next to one. Finding a safer place is not a matter of choice. The whole country rumbles and jitters as though it were balancing precariously atop a circus bear's unicycle.

To this, the Japanese are amazingly resigned. To live here is to know all too well the unsettling feeling of an earthquake's sudden jolt and to feel that split second of intense fear that this time it might be the Big One when the walls come crashing down.

So the Japanese have chosen to look for a silver lining. Archeological digs indicate that some of the earliest settlements were located near natural thermal wells. The warmth of the waters was used for cooking, for protection against the cold, and, undoubtedly, for bathing. Today, crowded spas can be found on the rims of very ominous-looking volcanoes, where the rotten-egg smell of sulfur is almost unbearable and some of the gurgling springs too hot to enter. The pungent spas of Mount Unzen, whose eruption in the 1990s killed nearly fifty people (mostly photojournalists), are once again overflowing with tourists.

Aficionados have likened the hot springs to oil in the Middle East, seeing the tens of thousands of gushing wells nationwide as Japan's greatest natural blessing, their healing and soothing powers all the more poignant because they are the flip side of the country's inescapable natural curse.

By going right to the source of their fears, the Japanese manage to escape. When they are done soaking up a tiny portion of the heat-energy that has been bestowed upon them, and are back in their famously disaster-prone cities, they move on to face another day, deliberately oblivious to the dangers dealt them by the gods of nature they have worshipped and feared for millennia.

EVERY NATION HAS its obsessions.

The blossoming of the cherries draws tens of millions of Japanese outdoors every spring for a few days—or a week, if the weather holds—of drinking, singing, and surprising displays of public abandon from an otherwise notoriously reserved bunch of people. The annual high school baseball championships are a summer ritual that commands the nation's attentions to an amazing degree. Most of the country mobilizes in the first three days of the new year to make prayers and buy lucky charms at Shinto shrines or Buddhist temples, and then again in August for the Festival of the Dead, when respects are paid to the ancestors.

Then there is bathing.

While the Japanese have adopted so much else wholesale, first from the Chinese and then the West, they have zealously guarded two important indigenous must-haves in the center of their existence. In their homes, there is still almost always a place by the door to leave your shoes before venturing further inside. And the bathroom really is a room for the bath. As a matter of convenience, the toilet is located nearby, but in a clearly separate space.

According to a survey conducted by Shiseido, a leading Japanese cosmetics company, in the mid-1990s, virtually all Japanese claimed to bathe (as opposed to shower) three or more times a week, while only about a quarter of all New Yorkers did. In reality, most Japanese bathe just about every day, if possible.

There are practical reasons for this. Japan's main island, Honshu, where most of the people live, has cold winters and hot, muggy summers. Just as the warmth of a bath is more deeply satisfying than a shower on a cold night, it is also extremely refreshing at the end of a sweat-drenched summer day.

But the relaxation factor can't be overemphasized. Surveys indicate Japanese men believe the bath is the most relaxing time they spend at home, more so than unwinding with a beer, chatting with their spouse, or playing with the children.

The tub isn't really intended as a place to get clean. That is done in the washing area outside of it, where one is expected to douse away all signs of shampoo or soap suds with the shower or with water scooped out of the bath in a special bucket. Once all the outer dirt is gone, one is free to climb into the tub to soak away the psychological toils of the day.

So sacrosanct is the purity of the tub that economy-minded housewives often recycle bathwater for use the next day in the washing machine, which is almost always located in an alcove adjacent to the bath in Japanese homes. Even after being used by the whole family, the water is that clean.

By keeping the bath itself clean, the water is available for more than one user—and the Japanese are famous for their long tradition of communal bathing, adding a dimension of social bonding to the bath that transcends its importance as a method of personal hygiene.

In 1591, Tokyo's first public bath, or *sento*, was opened by a man named Yoichi Ise, in what is now the rather drab, lower-middle-class Edobashi area; by the end of the seventeenth century they could be found everywhere. Writings from the time indicate the sento were dark places, closer to a sauna or steam room than the deep baths that are now the rule. The sexes more often than not bathed together, until the Japanese government was shamed by Western morality into pulling them apart in the late 1800s.

Before gender became an issue, distinctions of a more Japanese nature were enforced. Records at one of Japan's oldest hot springs resorts, Dogo, on the island of Shikoku, show that in 1635 the local overlord created separate sections for the samurai warrior caste, the Buddhist priesthood, and commoners.

By the end of the feudal era in 1868, there were six hundred bathhouses in Tokyo. There were an excess of twenty thousand nationwide in the mid-1960s, when cramped housing conditions forced millions of city dwellers to opt for the communal facilities their tiny apartments lacked. Today, as Japan's living standards have improved and city dwellers' ties to the community around them have loosened, the number of public baths has tumbled to about seven thousand, prompting the government to subsidize those that remain in an attempt to preserve what most would agree is an industry on its final legs.

In the home, meanwhile, the bath has remained a group endeavor. One tub of water is used by the whole family, and the plug isn't pulled until the last family member is done. Since the longer one has to wait the cooler the water is likely to be, guests were traditionally given first-dip rights, and who got the coveted first-in slot could be a good measure of a family's internal pecking order. (This has changed—most baths now have heaters to keep the water warm until everyone is done.)

Parents often bathe with their children until they are big enough to start kindergarten, or later in many cases. And it is the mark of the end of the honeymoon years of a marriage when a husband and wife no longer bathe together regularly.

Apartments designed for young singles are increasingly an exception to this rule. Having no one to soak with and little money to spend on rent, young people are more open to the idea of the "unit bath," a hotel-style bathroom with toilet, bath, shower, and wash basin all together in the same molded-plastic room.

A BASIC FACT of life: the more people take part, the more difficult it is to keep a bath clean. Infrequent cleaning of the communal tubs can spawn contamination by bacteria, including the variety that causes Legionnaire's disease. With the trend toward building larger—and thus harder to clean—baths to hold ever more paying bathers, this problem has become more pressing. Six people died in a hot springs resort during the Legionnaires outbreak in 2002, and each year the tribulations of hospitalized bathers are the subject of newspaper headlines.

Often, though, the bathers have only themselves to blame when a good bath goes bad. Heavy drinking and hot baths—a popular combination—are the beginning of hundreds of trips to emergency rooms each year. Both activities open the capillaries, bringing lots of blood up to the skin to cool, which is why drinking makes many people flush. But because the blood is diverted to the skin, there is less available to power other important organs, including the brain, and thus drunken bathers are doubly prone to passing out.

Alcohol and hot baths together can also speed a bather's pulse to the point that it becomes erratic, or even cause the heart to stop altogether. Warnings spelling out these dangers are posted in just about every changing room in the country.

But by that time, of course, they might as well be written in invisible ink. Intense reveling before, after, and sometimes during repeated immersions is de rigueur with group tours. Decanters of rice wine are even placed on floating platters by the very innkeepers who put up the warnings. It's been that way for centuries.

Even in the home, Japan's way of bathing has its dangers. Old people, in particular, are at risk—an ominous fact in a country that already has the world's longest life-expectancy for both men and women as well as perhaps the most rapidly aging population in the world.

According to a study done in 2003 for the Tokyo Metropolitan Institute of Gerontology by Ryutaro Takahashi, M.D., there were as many as fourteen thousand sudden deaths during bathing in 1999, making bathing a more dangerous activity than driving.

Most are listed simply as "at home drowning," with perhaps a footnote adding "cardiac arrest" or "cerebral attack." Takahashi noted that it isn't a matter of old folks slipping and hitting their heads. It's the water. The Japanese tendency to completely submerge all of the body but the head—in water at temperatures of 108°F and above—strongly affects blood pressure and the concentration of blood in the brain, heart, and lungs. Sudden changes from a cold dressing room to a hot bath, or prolonged exposure to hot water and the pressure its weight exerts on the organs, are especially dangerous for the elderly and, in Takahashi's opinion, present a "serious health issue."

"The number of deaths during bathing appears to be enormous," he wrote, before concluding his report with this intriguing bit of trivia: About as many Japanese die in their baths, he says, as Greeks drown in accidents at sea.

HOT SPRING RESORTS are a prime example of the bath as a bastion of traditional values—a place to be openly and unabashedly Japanese. They are, for example, the only places where people who aren't professional sumo wrestlers can still spend most of the day dressed in traditional robes called *yukata*, which are otherwise only worn for summer festivals or a handful of other special events. In Ikaho, like most hot springs resorts, visitors arrive in their suits or jeans and quickly change into the robes provided by the *ryokan*, the traditional inns, which, in sharp contrast with the commercial lodgings everywhere else, are built according to traditional aesthetics.

Inside the rooms are tatami mats, floor cushions instead of chairs, and futon beds that stay neatly tucked away in the closets until sunset. Dinners are almost exclusively in the classic style of Japanese cuisine, with a parade of dishes that often seem to be selected more for their color, local importance, or seasonal nuances than for their taste.

It's almost an identity thing. Though the vast majority of Japanese live in the cities, there is a strong undercurrent of nostalgia for the countryside. For many, hot springs resorts, often located in out-of-the-way places, have come to embody the image of the rustic beauty of the "real" Japan, the spiritual motherland that flourished before the West came flooding in.

Ikaho is an easy day trip from Tokyo, just a couple hours by train. But, psychologically, it is centuries away from the city. Any city. And very deliberately so. That's part of the hot springs' function—experts say just the change of scenery is a major element in a hot springs retreat's power to heal.

So, though scandalized by the revelations of tampering in 2004, it turned out that most Japanese weren't deterred from including trips to hot springs in their vacation plans. Like the man who puts women on a pedestal of perfection and yet wants to rip their clothes off at the same time, the Japanese both worship and thoroughly enjoy their water.

When I was in Ikaho at the height of the tampering tempest, everyone was talking about the scandal. But few of the people I spoke with, outside of the more idealistic innkeepers and bath critics, seemed to be at all outraged.

Sure, it was disconcerting, the tourists would tell me, when pressed. Terrible, really. There should be some arrests. But, you know, the hot springs experience is so much more than bathing. The village is so pretty. And it was great to get out of the city and away from the office, if only for a day or two. Plus, the food!

"I don't even really know what's supposed to be in the water," one unabashedly unconcerned young woman on an overnight package trip from Tokyo told me. "All the minerals and stuff. It just feels good because it's hot."

So there you have it. Like the tea ceremony or a session of Zen meditation, the Japanese bath is, at its best, a celebration of the beauty of the transcendent. It exposes that intangible sublime something that emerges when human activity, physical and mental, is consciously, carefully stripped down to its bare essentials.

But much more than Zen or the tea ceremony could ever be, the bath is the melting pot of Japanese culture. It's an honest expression of life. Not only is the bath where the Japanese come clean, it's also where they bare themselves to the world.

Where, as Tamura said, they come to cleanse their souls.

iv

II

THE SCIENCE OF IT

A boat journey to Shikine Island
for a dip in one of Japan's most remote onsen
and a stay in an odorous tent.
Where do these hot springs come from?
What's in them and what does the water do to us?

I HAVE LOST ALL track of time.

There is a patch of open sky above me, and through the mesh entrance of my tent I can see that it is full of stars. Directly over me is a sparkling Cygnus. Still rising in the east, the nearly full moon backlights several pine trees along the trail to my cul-de-sac campsite. At most 150 feet away, I can hear waves breaking on the beach at the bottom of the scrub-covered dune I share with maybe a dozen other people, all of whom are now finally quiet.

Although they are the harbingers of an incoming storm, I welcome the gusty breezes and the on-again, off-again pattering of the rain, if nothing else than for the distraction they provide from the buzzing of a particularly aggressive mosquito and the flutterings of a mysterious but clearly much larger bug that has been flying sorties into my airspace since sundown.

A strong metallic smell fills my tent. That would be me. I have been bathing all day in carbonated pools of diluted iron sulfide.

Because of the vagaries of the Japanese bureaucracy, I am technically still in Tokyo. But, with nearly 125 miles of ocean between us, Tokyo and I are a world apart. So far apart that back in Japan's feudal days the shogunate rulers in the capital, then still called Edo, used this secluded island and its neighbors as a dumping ground for criminals and other public enemies they chose to exile from society. Now, the whole chain is a national park. And a dumping ground for Tokyo's tourists.

I am on Shikinejima, the fourth of the Izu Islands, a string of volcanoes that stretches from Oshima, about seventy-five miles southeast of Tokyo, to the distant and tiny Aogashima, which is little more than a gaping caldera some two hundred miles out to sea.

Little known and barely inhabited, the islands are located in one of the world's most happening seismological zones. Below them, two tectonic plates crash into each other like a couple of trains colliding head-on—except at an imperceptibly slow pace and with immeasurably more energy. It is this eternal struggle on this seaward detour from the Pacific's Ring of Fire that lights up the Izu volcanoes and rocks the islands with numbingly frequent, bone-rattling earthquakes. Because it is lighter, the northern edge of the Philippine plate tends to get the better deal, forcing the western edge of the Pacific plate down and under. In some places, the plate seems to go almost straight down. The deepest place on the surface of the Earth, the Marianas Trench, is located along the same subjugation line, and drops off more than seven miles.

Like most of the people on Shikine, I came by ship. My journey began early in the morning at the Tokyo pier of the Tokai Kisen Co. Ltd, which seems to have a corner on all sea travel to the Izu islands. Tidy and a bit out of the way, the terminal is busy, but not crowded. Ships with names like the *SS Sarubia* or the *SS Camelia* pull in and steam away again throughout the day, chugging across Tokyo Bay and then over the horizon into the Pacific. Though the rides can be long and taxing—the slow boat to Shikine takes about seven hours, and all landings are at the mercy of the waves—the mood at the Tokai Kisen pier always seems festive and expectant. Maybe a tad nervous too.

As a reminder that nature is out there, ready to pounce, the convenience store at the terminal stocks gas masks. I didn't bring it with me, but I have one from an earlier Izu trip, when they were required of all passengers going to Miyakejima, which was just then being slowly repopulated after a volcanic eruption in 2000 forced the evacuation of the entire island. Five hundred homes were destroyed by ash and mudslides, and to this day whole neighborhoods remain half buried, à la Pompeii, in ten-foot-deep flows of black basalt.

No one was killed that September, but the four thousand-plus islanders weren't allowed to return to Miyake for the next five years because, while the most spectacular pyrotechnics had long subsided, the volcano continued to spit up smoke and poisonous gas. When I went there with the second wave of returning villagers, whole swaths of Miyake remained off limits and a white plume rising from the crater at the center of the island hung ominously above us. When the wind blew just so, the sulfur in the air was enough to make my eyes water and my throat pucker.

It was a sad visit. Frustrated by their seemingly endless life in limbo, many of the island's younger residents called it quits and found more stable soil in which to put down their roots. But with nowhere else to go, or simply out of loyalty to the volcano of their birth, their grandparents were more likely to stick it out. So Miyake, once one of the most popular islands in the Izu chain, had become something of an old folks' home.

Unlike the restive Miyake just to the north, there hasn't been an eruption on Shikine in more than a thousand years, and that was actually on what is now a separate and larger island, Niijima. The catastrophic Genroku Earthquake of December 31, 1703, created a waterway between Shikine and Niijima and also killed some ten thousand people, many as far away as the capital. But while the Shikine of today may be something of an oddity in the Izus because it doesn't have a crater to call its own, it does share one major trait with all the other isles—it's got a very active underground.

After arriving at the island's port, on its northern tip, I hiked to its southeast coast, a walk that took all of twenty minutes. Shikine is truly tiny—with a circumference of just seven-and-a-half miles. But it is bursting with life. My hike was repeatedly punctuated by the sound of plump, pointy-headed grasshoppers, all bright green, jumping clumsily into the roadside brush to avoid being stepped on. There were rainbow-striped lizards sunning themselves, and dust-colored spiders as big as my hand, but paper-thin. The island is a bird sanctuary, and in the spring its rugged coasts go white under flocks of black-tailed gulls there to lay eggs and raise their chicks.

Just beyond a little marina on the southeast shore, I passed a red and yellow sign warning all visitors to quickly vacate the area if an earthquake struck, since it would likely be inundated by any resulting tsunami. I shrugged off the warning and continued on my way. With the water in front of me and a cliff at my back, there was obviously nowhere else to quickly go. In a few minutes, I crossed through a rocky arch and found my first Shikine hot springs. Actually, I almost missed them.

Boiling-hot water bubbles up from below the shores of Shikine and for the most part the islanders have left it to its natural flow. The island's signature hot springs, the Ashitsuki Onsen, are just a conveniently arranged collection of rocks that form several thigh-deep pools in a tide-pool-pocked strip of coastline. Just a touch of cement has been added to smooth the way.

The temperature of the pools depends on the tide—the more seawater gets mixed in, the cooler they are.

Legend has it that the baths were discovered by islanders who happened to see an injured sea lion, or *ashika*, healing itself there.

About ten minutes away by foot, a narrow, dead-end road through the woods opens up to a deep ravine, and at the bottom of a steep flight of rocky stairs, dug out of another craggy shore, is Jinata hot springs. Things can get real hot around here; bathers are encouraged to check just how hot the water is at Jinata, which means "earth hatchet," before they get in. It's sound advice. Though one of Shikine's more imaginative travel campaigns described Jinata's core temperature level of around 176°F as "toasty," skin begins to scald at about 120°F. Luckily, enough seawater usually washes into the tide pools to create pockets that won't boil bathers alive.

For better or worse, bathing doesn't get much more primal than this. And it's not necessarily an amusement for the squeamish. Swarms of ancient-looking sea lice, the seashore's answer to the cockroach, line the rims of the pools, scampering away only when the approach of a human form becomes apparent to their woefully near-sighted compound eyes. And the bottom of one of the more scenic springs near Ashitsuki was covered by a thin film of slick, reddish-brown muck, residue of the highly concentrated and odorous iron sulfides that are Shikine's trademark.

Despite repeated dunks in the ocean, the stink of these pools stayed with me for days after I left the island.

ABOUT 670,000 GALLONS of water gush from Japan's hot springs every minute.

That's an awful lot of water. But the total volume of water on the Earth is 330 million cubic miles. If you were to take all of the water and somehow

v

launch it into outer space to form an aquaplanet, it would have a diameter of 840 miles, more than one-half the size of Pluto, or one-third of the moon. About 96 percent of the water on Earth is saline, ocean water. Of the fresh-water, 68 percent is frozen in ice caps or glaciers and 30 percent—or about 2.5 million cubic miles—is in the ground. Rivers, lakes, and streams are a surprisingly sparse resource, making up only about 0.015 percent of all the water on Earth. Biological water, the stuff in living things like us, by the way, accounts for a miniscule 0.0001 percent.

The amount of water gushing up in Japan's hot springs comes out to 0.6 cubic miles, or 0.0000002 percent of all the fresh underground water on the planet. So, no, Japan's hot springs enthusiasts aren't hogging all the world's bath water.

But there's still an awful lot of water gushing out of the ground in this country. Enough, easily, for more than 120 million people to bathe in each year and to keep the 25,565 mineral springs—with an average temperature of 107°F (which *is* actually nice and toasty)—well lubricated year-round.

Most of it comes from rain, in keeping with the water cycle—evapo-ration, condensation, precipitation, et cetera—that we all learned about as kids in school. Rain and melted snow or ice water, naturally inclined by gravity to keep moving down, infiltrate the ground. The farther down the water goes, the warmer it becomes, due to the increasing heat and pressure of the earth's crust. When it gets warm enough, it starts moving up again, and more cool water will push its way down to continue the cycle.

But once the water is underground, getting out again can be a fantastically slow process. There are lots of nooks and crannies where it can get stuck. With the advanced drilling techniques now in use, researchers believe some Japanese baths are pulling up water that has been trapped in subterranean aquifers, ripening, one might say, for thousands or even millions of years.

Physicist Tetsuo Miyazaki, who after retiring from a teaching position at Nagoya University has become one of the leading experts on such wells, says his research suggests baths in the Nobi Plains of central Japan could be filled with water dating back to the Miocene epoch, making it as much as 16 million years old.

"This was before humans in their present form even existed, in the time of the desmostylia, the forerunner of the elephant, and other large mammals," he explained to me after presenting a paper at a scholarly conference devoted to new developments in the study of hot springs. "It's fascinating to soak in the actual waters of that era before man and imagine what that world was like."

Because this fossil water—paleowater, in the jargon of the initiated—is, like fossil fuel, a limited resource that can't be replaced, at least not without investing a few millennia, pumping it up is sometimes likened to mining, and a scattered few concerned environmental groups are beginning to make an argument for conservation.

Such filtration baths are relatively rare, however. Usually, it's the energy of volcanism that brings the waters up, no need for drills or pumps. Japan, an archipelago of volcanoes, is one big water heater. The country's fault-line-ridden topography also plays well into the hot springs picture, offering a sort of delivery system for getting the water to the surface.

Temperature is certainly important, but that's not what the real hot springs connoisseur cares about. It's not the water, so much, as what's in the water. Japan's deliberately liberal Hot Springs Law, drawn up with the interests of the tourist industry firmly in mind, allows for wells with temperatures as low as 77°F at the source, which would actually make for a pretty chilly dip.

But to qualify as a hot spring, a well must also contain a certain amount of any of about eighteen substances or gasses, ranging from strontium (used to put the red color in flares and fireworks) to hydro-arsenic acid. It doesn't even have to be a whole lot. Only one milligram per kilogram of lithium, for example, will do the trick.

Like good wine, each bath has its own character. Carbon-dioxide baths bubble up when you get in, kind of like a fresh Coke would if you swished your finger around in it. Sulfur baths, very common on and around volcanoes, smell like rotten eggs and often have a yellowish buildup along their rims. Iron-heavy water, like that in the hot springs of Shikine, looks transparent as it comes out of the ground, but oxidizes into a reddish-brown when it hits the air. Calcium baths have a distinctive milky color. And then there are the ever-popular radioactive baths.

What will be in the water depends on how hot it is—and thus how much mineral it can absorb to begin with—and what kinds of rocks it came through on its way out of the ground. Most hot springs are colorless and odorless, or of the sodium-chloride variety. Simply put, that means they are either just hot and wet, or just hot, wet and salty. Still, experiments have established that, compared with tap water, the basic salty combination does work to magnify the power of the waters to heat a bather up, bringing the warmth deeper into the body and keeping it there longer. The primary reason for this is that the salt, or other minerals, on the skin makes it harder for sweat to evaporate, allowing the bather to, literally, simmer in his or her own juices.

A lot of attention, especially in the New Age and alternative medicine circles, has been focused in recent years on the health benefits of the negative ion environment common in hot springs areas.

Ions are charged particles in the air created by the ejection of an electron from a molecule. The molecules that have lost their electron take on a positive electrical charge, and are thus called positive ions. When the displaced electron finds a new molecule to attach itself to, a negative ion is born.

Negative ions tend to be found in forests and settings with running or falling water, such as the seashore, where the crashing of the waves acts to break up the water molecules. One of the reasons people enjoy walking in the woods or relaxing on the beach might be the higher concentration of negative ions around them. Negative ion advocates, in fact, go so far as to call their charges the "vitamins of the air."

On the flip side, high levels of positive ions are often associated with air pollution. Some researchers—the ones most likely to be quoted by companies marketing air purifiers–even argue that positive ions may be behind folk beliefs that evil "witch" winds, such as the Foehn that blows across Switzerland and southern Germany or the Mistral of southern France, bring with them crime, depression, and all kinds of other social and physical ills.

The final litmus test of a bath is, well, the litmus test. A bath with waters registering a pH factor of 7 is considered neutral. The closer it moves to 1, the more acidic it is. Anything from 7 to 14 is alkaline. Healthy humans tend to be slightly alkaline, with a pH reading of just over 7. Most Japanese baths fall into roughly the same alkaline category, with a smooth feel that makes them soothing to soak in. Acidic waters, on the other hand, are generally pungent, have a harsher feel, and are effective at killing bacteria.

Which brings us back to me. And my skin.

I AM—AS ALL OF US are by design—dead on the outside.

We are covered by what dermatologists call the *stratum corneum epidermidis*, the "layer of corn," a thin (about .04 of an inch) covering of the keratin remains of flattened, dried out, and very dead skin cells. Every minute,

vi

we shed thirty thousand or more of them. Every month, we get a whole new coat, just as lifeless as the last.

But that doesn't mean our birthday suit is barren territory. When we think of ourselves, we tend to forget that we are a minority in our own bodies. Healthy adult humans have a larger population of microflora on and in us than we have cells of our own. It's not even a close contest. In our guts alone, the number of bacteria—without which we would die—is higher than the number of mammalian cells that comprise what we would normally consider to be the essential us. And about one trillion bacteria inhabit our skin—an infestation of Biblical proportions when one remembers there are only six billion people on mother Earth.

A typical square-inch of skin is not only a staggeringly complex ecosystem, but it has some pretty amazing plumbing of its own—about 19 million cells, 625 sweat glands, 90 oil glands, a few dozen hair follicles, 1200-plus pain receptors, a dozen cold and 80 heat receptors, and 13 feet of blood vessels. As we've already established, bacteria rule, and on that one inch will flourish dozens and dozens of different varieties, including throngs of *staphylococci* and *streptococci* (think staph infections and strep throat) and *corynebacteria*, strains of which every now and then (most often with the unwitting help of a dentist) find their way into the bloodstream, form "vegetations" on heart valves, and kill their hapless hosts. The warmer and moister the locale, the happier the camping. Thus runny noses, athlete's foot, and jock itch. Few bacteria bother with the drier, less hospitable areas of the back.

But bacteria are just one of the many tribes to whom we play host. We're also crawling with mites and other parasites, and the fungi love us. And how could they resist? The skin is a very special organ. It is where we and the world meet. As our outer wrapping, it provides the face and substance to whatever we may see ourselves to be on the inside, and to what others see us to be as well. It is as deep as beauty goes. Beyond it, the intangible begins. No boundary is more absolute.

In a more practical sense, the skin is also the body's first line of defense against invasion, its heater and cooler, and its primary detector of pain and pleasure. In many ancient civilizations, where actually cutting into the body for a look around was frowned upon, the skin was regarded as both a barometer of what is happening with our internal organs and as a cooperative medium through which poultices and other medicines could slowly seep.

Then the idea of impermeability gained favor. Slicing open the sick became an art. Poultices and patches were put aside as physicians sought instead to administer drugs through whatever ready openings could be found. Hypodermic needles and X-rays removed the skin from the equation altogether. Until just a few decades ago, this view of the skin as a strong barrier against the outside world, waterproof and largely impervious to chemical infiltration, held firm.

But as I sat in the springs of Shikine, my own skin was telling me there was something seriously wrong with that idea.

There's a lot of give and take going on in a bath. For one thing, millions of those bacteria that were on me when I went in weren't going to ever make it out again. And a good number of my dead skin cells would be keeping them company. But the transaction is much more fundamental than that.

Due to diffusion and osmosis, I will either take a bit of the bathwater with me when I go, or I will leave a bit of my own body water behind. Contrary to the more seemingly logical assumption that, like a prune, wrinkling up means you are drying out, you pucker in the bath because you are taking on water. It accumulates between the stratum corneum and the layer of the epidermis below it, causing the wrinkles.

This only occurs if you have a saltier constitution than the water around you. Just as surely as a body of water will flow downward, it will also seek equilibrium in the amount of stuff dissolved inside it. So if, for example, you are in the ocean—or in a hot spring with lots of saltwater in it—you will dry out a little bit as the water in you and the seawater try to coordinate their salinity levels. The relatively pure water in your body seeps out to dilute the much saltier waters around you (or, to put it another way, as you absorb the salt from the ocean, you lose a slight amount of water in the trade-off). It is because our cells are semi-permeable—neither impervious nor utterly vulnerable—that this can happen. Our cell walls are able to regulate how much, but they do allow a small amount of water to get in or out.

Pretty much the same goes for the minerals in the water. Were the Shikine baths of a higher concentration, the impermeability concept wouldn't matter much. Toxicity would take over. The chemicals would overwhelm my skin's defenses, in this case most likely causing rashes and scratchy eyes. That's still getting off pretty easy, though. Just try drinking it. Ingesting as little as five grams of this particular chemical highball can cause vomiting and abdominal pain. Slightly higher amounts of iron sulfide have been known to destroy the liver, induce shock and/or comas, and even result in death.

Some of the other common hot springs solvents are equally toxic. Arsenic comes to mind. Bromide, an ingredient in ethylene dibromide, a lead scavenger used to purify gasoline, causes painful sores when spilled on the skin.

I, however, am immersed in a safely watered-down mixture. The springs feel decidedly soft. They are calming. And I can rest assured in the added knowledge that there is a whole branch of medicine, balneotherapy, dedicated to understanding what is going on with my body right now.

One of its leading practitioners, professor emeritus Yuko Agishi of the Hokkaido University School of Medicine, believes the "bath cure" involves three main elements: the effects of the heat of the water on the body, the effects of the minerals in the water, and the psychological benefits of the spa environment itself.

"In today's stressful and aging society, balneotherapy can be used effectively not only for treatment of chronic diseases and rehabilitation, but also for preventing life-habit-related diseases which cannot be cured by drug therapy," he wrote in a recent paper explaining the practice of spa medicine in Japan.

In the doctor's opinion, the mere heat of the water, when over about 107°F, increases the production of hormones and stimulates the immune system. Hot-spring bathing, he said, has significant therapeutic powers in the reduction of inflammation and pain, and it can offer remedies or at least relief from such maladies as rheumatoid arthritis, bronchial asthma, and diabetes mellitus.

Virtually every hot spring in Japan claims to cure something. The Shikine springs, because of their high iron and sulfur content, are supposed to be good for gastrointestinal troubles, neuralgia, rheumatism, the symptoms of menopause, and speeding along the healing of cuts and scrapes.

In general, balneologists break down the potential therapeutic factors of a bath by its more common minerals. Sulfates, for instance, are seen as good for the circulation, heart disease, high blood pressure, and impotence. Calcium helps with stomach problems and allergies. Magnesium is good for the skin. The most common baths, high in salt, are useful in treating bronchial disorders and diabetes.

But here's the bad news. For most hot-spring bathers, this is all academic.

According to Agishi and most other balneotherapists, the effects of the bath take at least a few weeks to really set in. He believes a well-scheduled daily routine of repeated but regular immersions is required for a bath to be truly beneficial; he suggests that the use of hot springs be seen more as a long-term step toward developing a healthy lifestyle that prevents disease, rather than a quick cure for those that have already cropped up.

So much for the healing powers of the day dip.

But there's something we haven't added into the mix yet.

IT'S JUST ABOUT IMPOSSIBLE to find a crowd on Shikine.

Only six hundred people actually live there. Nearly all of the roughly forty thousand tourists who come each year come in July or August, but the total number of people on the island never exceeds three thousand.

As I hiked around the island at the very tail end of the summer season, I realized that I was well above the average age of the tourists around me. High school and college students on summer excursions were the norm. There were some young couples and small groups of young women, dressed in heels and, alas, carrying their de rigueur Chanel or Louis Vuitton bags. I saw a few married pairs with toddlers. My fellow campground dwellers were seasoned backpackers, most of them in their early thirties.

These tourists come for the beaches, not the baths. Unlike many of the other Izu islands, where the shores are covered in coarse, black volcanic sand, Shikine's beaches are buried under a blanket of glass beads, with some coral mixed in for balance. Its coastal waters are as alive as its inner hills, with everything from yellow jacks to chubs to nibblers to parrot and puffer fish. Farther out, whales and dolphins ply the waters, and flying fish are a common sight alongside the Tokai Kisen fleet.

Everything is just a few minutes' walk from everything else. There are no trains. No subways. I didn't see a TV, nor did I read a newspaper the whole time I was there. When I asked a shopkeeper when her grocery store would close, she told me whenever the customers stopped dropping in.

For sunset, I had a cove to myself. Not only was I the only bather at the Ashitsuki springs, I was probably the only human within a couple of kilometers. And we have now arrived at item three on Dr. Agishi's balneology list: the healing power of simply getting away from it all.

The feel-good factor of bathing in a hot springs is magnified by the fact that just getting to them requires making a deliberate escape, however brief, from the daily routines of life. Even when a hot spring has been drilled out of the ground in the middle of the city, the space surrounding it is almost always designed to look rustic and outdoorsy, the waters contained in wooden tubs overlooking veranda gardens or flowing into pools lined by irregularly shaped rocks. Whenever possible, there will be open-air bathing facilities. This is also probably why hot springs inns, with their relentless emphasis on the Japanese aesthetic, are so utterly different in concept from the country's equally ubiquitous Western-style hotels, which at the upper end of the scale do, after all, serve a similar purpose. Both strive to take their guests into a state of suspended animation, to deposit them as far away from their workaday worlds as possible. Hot springs resorts just happen to aim at doing that by plunking them down outside, in the nature they abandoned in the distant past, or to a Japan that, for most intents and purposes, vanished long, long ago.

Bobbing on the waves of an approaching typhoon, I felt vastly refreshed on the boat home from Shikine. Of course, returning from exile in Izu is much easier than it used to be. Though almost never used, the island has a helipad. And along with the slower steamers, Tokai Kisen began a daily jet foil route to and from Tokyo in 2002, cutting the travel time to just over two hours.

Weather permitting, that is. Much to the dismay of a couple hundred of my fellow travelers, the early boat was the first and last to leave Shikine that day. The ocean was getting too whipped up.

♨

As we pushed off to sea, with the sky a heavy gray and the waves splashing up over the deck, I remembered reading somewhere that the progression from life to death can be regarded as a matter of dehydration. It has been said that we are all just sacks of animated water.

Perhaps. But we are porous souls. Our private stash of water is constantly trying to escape from us and move on. In our lifetimes, we go from 95 percent water as fetuses to as much as 85 percent as infants, then to around 60 percent as adults (women tend to be a few percentage points lower than men) and finally down to about 55 percent when we are coming down the final stretch.

Even so, as I watched Shikine fade into the misty horizon I felt certain that, despite having just wantonly dipped into my own cellular reservoir, I had managed to set the whole process back somehow. Even if by just a drop or two.

銭湯大スキ
湯気の中はみんなしあわせ

東京都公衆浴場業環境衛生同業組合

III

SO GOES
THE NEIGHBORHOOD

From the bath down the street
to mass bathing facilities where water comes in many forms,
bubbly to electrified.
How the centuries-old sento may soon be a thing of the past.

GOING INTO A neighborhood bath for the first time is kind of like breaking and entering when you know the owners are home. It requires a certain amount of courage. Or naiveté. Or desperation.

I mean, look at me. I've lived within spitting distance of my *sento,* or public bath, for a decade, but I haven't been to it. Never had much cause to. I've got a bath. A pretty fine bath, in fact. And I don't have to share it with strangers.

When I was in college here, and living in a small dormitory, I had to share a bathroom with three roommates. When our schedules clashed, or when the mold got really nasty in the summer, I would occasionally walk down the street to the local bath. It was a small, nondescript place, so my memories are few.

I remember being splashed by a chubby Japanese father washing off his squirmy little boy. I remember getting loud and silly with friends there. But that's about it. It wasn't much to write home about. And I managed to stay away from public bathhouses for at least twenty years.

But I'm back. As I nervously brush back the indigo curtains that hang over the door to my neighborhood bathhouse and take off my shoes in the entranceway, I have the unshakable sensation that I am warping back into the 1960s. I slide open another set of doors and my premonition is confirmed—it is as though I have just entered a time capsule.

It's a bigger space than I expected and more like a living room, or a salon, than a place to undress. The tatami mats on the floor are brown with age and the tattered throw rugs on top of them look like something from my childhood home. They remind me, in fact, of the rugs that we used to give to the cats after they had fallen below our human standards.

The walls are made of dark, brown wood and are covered with photos of marathon runners taken at an annual race that passes by on the main street right in front of the bathhouse. The pictures look like they were taken at the inaugural race, which would have been decades ago.

Tacked up above the photos, higher up on the wall, is a line of posters. The selection is eclectic. There's a poster put out by the fire department urging all good citizens to make sure they've turned off the gas before they go to bed. There are a couple big, glossy posters with pretty women in kimono. "We love the bathhouse," said one. Then there is a big AIDS awareness poster, warning that it's *not* somebody else's problem.

That one seems ominously out of place, I think to myself. But, then again, I'm probably the only one noticing these details anyway.

ON THE OTHER SIDE of the room, there's a bunch of dusty old paper cranes hanging in a corner, and a calendar that has inspirational resolutions written down for each day. It uses only Chinese numbers. The year on it isn't 2006 but the traditional Japanese equivalent: Year of His Majesty, Heisei 18.

It seems so, well, ancient. The wall to my right is covered with coin lockers. There are keys, but I can tell that no one uses them. There are a couple of lumpy couches, both covered with white sheets and one partially covered by an old man in white long johns puffing on a cigarette. Between the couches is a low table on which there are jars of peanuts and rice crackers, free for the taking. There's a massage chair with two big knobs sticking out at shoulder level that are covered in orange towels.

I am guessing the chair has been broken since the reign of His Majesty, Emperor Showa.

The centerpiece of it all, the bath, is beyond a set of sliding glass doors on the far side of the room. A partition runs down the middle of the bath and dressing room, keeping the men's and women's sides separate. It's a somewhat half-hearted partition, though. The feeling of spaciousness in the room is due in large part to the ceiling, which is easily high enough to house a couple of floors. But the partition only goes about ten feet up, leaving a sense of connectedness with the other side. Though the view is obscured, anything said on one side is heard just as clearly on the other.

Right inside the entrance is the seat for the *bandai*, the attendant who collects your entry fee. The bandai sits facing toward the bath on a raised platform so that he or she has a clear shot at the changing rooms on either side. To thwart Peeping Toms, the seat is carefully positioned so that it is the only place that offers such a view.

When I went in, the bandai was a bemused old woman with her gray hair up in a frayed bun. (Men can be bandai. But not often.) She silently looked me over, smiling gently, until I said hello.

"Welcome," she said. "It's ¥400. Take whichever locker you please." She

then went back to watching the news on a large-screen TV.

So, in keeping with a venerable Japanese tradition far beyond me to question or criticize, she played the role of a watchful old lady—a neighbor in fact—supervising as I stripped down and sashayed over to the bath.

It is also customary in Japanese bathhouses for the walls to be tiled, and for the tiles to be arranged in elaborate mosaics. Mount Fuji is almost always the inspiration. And so it was in my neighborhood bath.

I hadn't expected anything noteworthy. From the outside, this bathhouse is not very promising. The entrance is small and the rickety wooden structure looks pretty much like any other old house in that—and just about any other—quiet residential area in Tokyo and its many suburbs. The curtain over the door, and the smokestack out back, are the only giveaways.

The dressing room pretty much confirmed my low expectations. But the bath was a sight to see. As I stood there naked, the mosaic before me covered the length and height of the far wall. Its tiles sparkled in their bright greens, reds, and blues. It began on the men's side with a seascape, a forest-covered emerald island, and a smaller framed-off area that depicted a completely different mountain scene, one that reminded me somehow of Switzerland. Over the partition, on the women's side, I could see Fuji itself, in all its symmetrical, snow-covered glory.

I had to admit, this was nice. Clean and bright. It drew me inside.

At about knee level were three rows of faucets, one hot and one cold for each washing station. In the corner was a stack of plastic buckets and stools. I grabbed one of each, washed the stool off, sat down, dumped a couple bucketfuls of hot water over my head and started lathering up.

After washing all the suds off myself, I climbed into the bath and realized that I had underestimated this place in another way as well. This bath was—excuse me—fucking hot. I mean really fucking *hot*.

I realized the bath was divided into two sections. Thinking I had made a novice's blunder, I hastily got out and climbed into the other side. It was just as hot.

It wasn't a huge bath, maybe the size of about six or seven household tubs. But it was quite deep, so the idea was to sit on a ledge that ran along the edge. Nevertheless, I was up to my chest. I lifted my arm and it was already red. My head started to swim.

To distract myself, I read a list of "don'ts" on the wall. It started out pretty much as I had expected—Don't come into the bath covered in soap; Don't shave or wash your hair in the bath—but toward the end, it started getting kind of weird and arcane—Don't do your laundry in the bath; Don't disobey the Public Health Law Regarding Public Bathing.

I was only able to stay in for about five minutes. The old guy in the long johns was still lounging around when I got out. Another skinny man was slowly getting dressed and watching sumo wrestling on the TV with the old woman and her husband, who shares the bandai duties.

I bought a bottle of milk coffee. The other two men were also drinking bottles of milk. It's one of those things that Japanese do when they bathe. We cheered on the wrestlers for a while. Then we finished getting dressed and headed out into the night.

As I walked home, I realized that I had just had the quintessential sento experience. And, despite myself, I had enjoyed it. I was clean and smelled nice. I was kind of warm inside, I had seen an aspect of my neighborhood that I had overlooked before, and the cold winter air felt good on my skin.

But there was no doubt in my mind that this bath, and the thousand or so others like it around Tokyo, would be gone before long. And I doubted if I would ever go back.

BATHHOUSES ARE NOT WITHOUT their fans. The Japanese government, for one, spends millions of yen each year propping up the industry. Without subsidies, a good portion of the baths like the one in my neighborhood would have evaporated years ago.

The rationale is similar to subsidies that are paid out to keep kabuki alive, or noh, or the bunraku puppet theater. It's a cultural thing. Whether the average Japanese person appreciates it or not, public bathhouses are a tradition, they are a part of this nation's history, and they deserve to be protected, preserved.

Or so the thinking goes. But it's not just that. Some people really like the baths.

Shinobu Machida likes them more than most. More than would be considered normal, in fact. A student of public bathhouses, he has over the past two decades visited more than two thousand of them across the nation, written books about them, and earned the nickname "Dr. Bath."

He has a pretty traditional take on the social value of public bathing. "There is something in the public bath that has been lost elsewhere in modern Japanese society," he says in the introduction to one of his books, *The Puzzle of the Public Bath.*

"When you are soaking in the bath, it melts the hardness away from your heart, and softens your emotions, making it easy for anyone to smile. This is the beginning of an exchange, of a contact. Even if it is just a momentary meeting of people who will never see each other again, it can be an instant in which there is a heart-to-heart communication."

Machida's books drip with nostalgia—and historical trivia. Public baths in the early days, for example, were dark places where the bathing area (more of a steam room) was separated from the dressing room by a low entrance, often only three feet or so high. This wasn't because people were shorter then, but because it helped contain the heat.

In the old days, the bathing areas for men and women were often separated by a partition only above the water, so that one could pass under it to get to the side reserved for the opposite sex. Dark and dangerous, such baths were not very big with the ladies. A more popular solution was one in which certain times were reserved for women, with men using the bath before or after.

And the word for Peeping Tom was, until fairly recently, *Depa-game*, the nickname of a man who in 1908 raped and murdered a woman after watching her bathe in Fuji no Yu, a public bathhouse in Tokyo.

He even offers an explanation for why Mount Fuji is on so many bathhouse walls. During the feudal period, when bathhouses really came into their own, the volcano was the object of a very popular religious cult that blended Buddhist and Shinto ideas and held Fuji to be a sort of paradise on Earth. Climbing Fuji, or simply coming in contact with it in some way, say by watching its likeness from the bath, was believed to bestow good luck and even salvation.

"You don't need to go to an amusement park," Machida writes in his bath book. "Go out and find your bathing wonderland."

But people like Machida, who see public bathhouses as both enjoyable and a treasure trove of Japanese tradition, are few and far between. And there is a touch of desperation in their defense of the local bathhouse custom.

Machida devotes a whole section of one of his books to how to find a good bath in an unfamiliar town, and then how to make the first visit as painless as possible. He admits that even as seasoned a bather as himself feels the embarrassment of that difficult debut: "All eyes are on you. You are a stranger. You are like a stray dog that has wandered into their house."

The rest of his advice tends to follow the same canine logic. Remember that you're not the boss dog, he says. Pick the least convenient locker, and wash in the spot closest to the door. "That's the worst place because that's where the cold wind comes in whenever somebody enters or leaves. So you won't be taking the best spot away from the regulars. And watch where they put their shoes."

From a business point of view, none of this can be good. Bathhouses are in desperate need of customers. Young, new customers. And that is exactly the people they are scaring away. As it was in my neighborhood bath, the regulars are few, and old. And basically everybody else, even college students, prefers to simply stay home.

No wonder the sento industry is drying up. According to the Tokyo Sento Association, the number of true public baths in the capital—the ones that fit the strictest definition of a sento, charge only ¥400 and are eligible for public assistance—has fallen from 2,687 in 1968 to just over 1000 in 2006.

This trend has been unrelenting for decades. The days when the local bathhouse will be harder to find than a Starbucks probably aren't far away. Introduced to Tokyo in 1996, there are about two hundred of the coffee shops in the capital now, a growth trend that is about as fast as is the sento's decline.

So dire are these straits that even Machida admits that extinction is a very real future scenario. "The days when people would come in crowds whatever you did are over," he wrote. "Public baths must change."

Funny thing is, they are. And in some amazing ways.

IN MY NEIGHBORHOOD, there are actually two public bathhouses. There's the regular one, which I've just described. And then there's the "Super Bath," called the Hot Water Fun House.

You can't miss it. Though it is off the main road on a back street surrounded by regular houses, much like the other bathhouse, the Hot Water Fun House is four stories tall and has a big billboard on the roof that is lit up by floodlights at night. It's open until one in the morning.

There is no curtain outside the automatic doors, which are up a flight of stairs on the second floor. There is no bandai inside. There is instead a reception desk, like you would expect in a hotel. It is staffed by middle-age women, who get no peeps at the male clientele sans clothes. Here, the men's and women's sides are separated not by a partition but by walls. Once you go into one or the other, there is no contact whatsoever with the opposite sex.

There is also no Mount Fuji mosaic. No public service announcements from the Fire Department. No old men lounging around in their skivvies.

But there *are* about a dozen baths.

The Hot Water Fun House and other *supaa sento*, as they are known, don't run on momentum or tradition. First-timers are welcome. When I made my first visit, just after the bath opened for the day on a snowy Sunday afternoon, I couldn't even tell who the regulars were. There were a few dozen men there, young, old, middle-age. There were kids. A guy with a golden earring. Nobody sat at the drafty washing stations up front. Nor did we give a damn where a regular might want to put his shoes.

The market principle is what keeps the customers coming in, and the aim is clearly to please. People don't come here because they need to get clean, or because they know the owners. They come because it's a sensual smorgasbord.

The basic price was the same as the other sento, ¥400. And there was no soap or shampoo here, oddly. But this was a three-for-one deal. Not only was there a regular hot and deep bath, there was also a bubbly bath and a sports bath, with massaging jets.

It was pretty nice. Soothing. And that wasn't all.

For an extra fee—and this is another big departure from the normal practice at traditional sento—bathers are given access to the "Royal Zone," a whole floor of additional bathing opportunities. There was a sauna, which had different herbal fragrances piped in depending on the day of the week; the ever-popular "water hang," a rope from which bathers could suspend themselves in various stages of immersion; spin baths, with jets that spun out bubbles for a very calming effect; and an outdoor bath set back in a rockscape on the roof of the building.

Offering a chance to lounge around naked in the middle of the city without the fear of arrest, the outdoor bath was especially popular. When I got in, I noticed that on a wooden deck next to the water there was the wet "shadow" of a man who had been sprawled out on it moments before.

Back inside, I tested out something called the "floating bath." I was intrigued by a sign next to it that said anyone getting in, no matter how heavy, would float. So I stretched out in its shallow waters and waited. And waited. And then noticed a big black button by my hand. When I pushed it, a barrage of bubbles attacked my underside.

Yep. I was floating. Cool.

But I was soon out of that and back on my feet. I had a few more things to try. One was the basic, cold bath. A classic. A staple. An ice cube. My toe went in first. Then, just to say I could, I jumped in, then jumped right back out again and ran out to the rooftop to heat up again. That bath was a comfortable 102°F. But that still wasn't all.

IN A CORNER OF THE commoners' zone, separated from the rest, was the "Hertz Bath."

I will say it right now: There is no bath that can compare. I'd been in one before and it took a bit of psyching up to do it again.

Perhaps you remember the kid's joke about the Hertz donut. The one where you ask the victim if he wants a Hertz Donut, and when he says "yes" you punch him in the arm and say, "Hurts, don't it?" Same idea.

The water was colored a light brown, just, I believe, to set this bath apart from the others. There was a sign above the bath with a long list of people who were requested to stay out. Anyone with a heart condition, for example. Children, pregnant women, epileptics, the hypertense. The list went on.

I understood why. But in the interest of getting my money's worth, I got in anyway.

The bath was shaped in a rectangle. Along the right and left sides were the white panels that emit the electricity. I walked to the back of the bath, about thigh-deep in the water, and felt nothing, which surprised me. So I bent over and stuck an arm in, up to the bicep. I immediately felt it. The electricity was pulsating through the water, and it tingled as it hit my skin. But it did more than that. It started to mess with my motor control. Soon my hand was curling back on itself, into a kind of claw.

But I wasn't beat quite yet.

Figuring I had that reaction because I had put my arm in too close to the panel, and having just watched in awe as a fellow bather sat immersed up to his neck in this bath for several minutes, I decided to assume the position. To do it right. Back up against the wall, body in middle, panels on either side.

I quickly lowered myself in. The pulsating was powerful. I felt it bouncing all through me. It both hurt and tickled. I couldn't figure out which, and that was the worst part of all. I just had this weird, not entirely pleasant, sensation all around and through me.

I got out after probably thirty seconds. If that. Though I love these things in theory, in practice it's a different story.

x

What a match. Water, electricity, and the human body. Just as we are all big sacks of saltwater, so are we, as Walt Whitman put it, "the body electric." It is electricity, racing through our nerves, that gives us pain and pleasure. It is the thoughts in our brain. It is produced in each of our cells.

There is enough electricity coursing through our bodies to light up a forty-watt lightbulb. And when our internal generator shuts down, we die.

Electrotherapy works on the basic idea that a controlled, outside source of electricity can be used to stimulate our cells into working more diligently. The approach can be hard or soft. Strong electric stimuli can force cells to behave differently, kind of the way your head works differently after being hit with a sledge hammer. Weak stimuli, on the other hand, can be used to "tickle" the cells. In the jargon of the experts, when I was in the Hertz bath I was participating in a session of "low-energy membrane tickling."

The stimulation is intended to speed cellular processes, such as cellular healing, and, using various delivery methods, is coming into wider and wider use in mainstream medical circles.

But don't try this at home. Water and electricity are a notoriously dangerous combination. According to Konishi Electric Co., Ltd, one of several companies that produce Hertz baths, also known simply as electricity baths, the baths are not fatal (or even dangerous) because the electric stimulation is low frequency and the amount of energy is carefully regulated, usually at from three to five volts.

That's not much. As a matter of fact, anything below fifty volts is what electricians call Extremely Low Voltage.

A small toaster or coffee maker will often operate on 220 volts. Throw that in the bath with you and you will start cooking. Before stricter safety regulations were created, small hand-held hair driers with about the same voltage killed dozens of people in showers and baths each year. At the other end of the spectrum, to ensure a very quick and certain death, the prisons in the United States that still use electric chairs generally set the voltage at about 2000 and the timers at fifteen seconds. Prison regulations in Nebraska, for example, call for a single jolt of 2,450 volts.

But what we are talking about here is more like the kind of power you need to operate a TV remote control than like "Riding the Lightning." AA batteries, the little thin ones that many remotes use, produce about 1.5 volts.

"Older people tend to like a stronger stimulus, but we prefer to keep it weak to satisfy as broad a group of customers as possible," Konishi says in its promotional materials.

Even so, one of the nasty things about electricity is that low voltage doesn't necessarily equal low hazard. The three main things that will determine whether you live or die are the amount of current flowing through your body (which is measured in amperes), what course the electricity takes when it passes through you, and how long you stay in the circuit.

You generally start to tingle when exposed to 1 milliampere. You feel a shock and start to lose the ability to pull away from about 6 or 7 milliamperes. When my hand started to curl up, because the electricity was forcing my muscles to contract, I could feel that I was starting to lose some freedom of movement.

But that's still pretty low-level exposure. The "let-go" zone—when you lose the ability to break free—actually goes up to about 30 milliamperes, depending on your muscle mass. Beyond that, you start pushing the limits. From 50 to 150 is where you get the severe pain, muscle contractions, respiratory failure. At 1,000 to 4,300 your heart loses its beat and nerves start to break down. At 10,000 the heart stops, death is likely, and severe burns appear.

Had I not been able to pull my hand away, even the low voltage of the bath could have caused me serious distress. But when I got in full body, I found the effect was greatly diminished. It was still uncomfortable. But it wasn't nearly as powerful, and I had no problem getting out again.

After I got out, I asked at the front desk if anyone had ever been shocked or otherwise injured by the electric baths. No, I was told, with a bit of a patronizing giggle. Konishi also claims the baths they produce are safe, noting that they are similar in power to popular massaging devices that are on the general market.

Could be. I've never heard of any accidents, there's no particular movement to ban them, and the popularity of the baths is amazing. Around since the 1940s—Konishi has been making them since 1963—electric baths are now almost de rigueur at Super Sento.

SO MACHIDA DID get it kind of right. Even in the bath, it's a dog-eat-dog world.

Traditional sento, clinging to the past and offering a service hardly anyone needs anymore, are vanishing. But the Super Sento, with their specialty baths, sprawling parking lots, and flashy billboards, have taken over the countryside. In many rural areas, they are the most popular thing to do in town after dark. And the concept—with a strong emphasis on sophistication—has also taken the cities by storm, with bath emporiums that stagger the imagination.

Tokyo has several huge bathing parks, the most impressive being LaQua. And it is impressive. Located next to the Tokyo Dome stadium and the Korakuen amusement park (and owned by the same company as both), the $141 million LaQua complex has its own shopping mall and roller coaster.

It may sound more like a nudist colony than a public bath, but no, you don't shop and squeal in the raw. Those pleasures are handled in the non-nude areas. Nevertheless, LaQua's spa is an amazing space. It spreads out over four floors, offering panoramic views of the city and all the flavors of bathing water one could wish for.

Of course, all those extras don't come cheap. LaQua's entrance fee is roughly six times the average sento. And that's just to get in the door. Its hours are also decidedly non-sento: 11:00 A.M. to 9:00 A.M. the following day, a schedule that reflects the fact that many of its guests are killing time after missing the last train home. And many of them wouldn't be caught dead in their local sento.

Another large bathing park, Toshimaen-Niwa-no-Yu, is part of another amusement park and one of Tokyo's biggest swimming pools on the other side of town. The main bath, surrounded by a Japanese garden, opened with much fanfare in the summer of 2003, and attracted somewhere around four hundred thousand guests in its first year.

It is hard to assess the growth of the Super Baths. There aren't any good figures for how many of them there are. Unlike the closely regulated sento, which have their own tightknit community and industry associations, the Super Baths are pretty much fishing around on their own. They are required to comply with stringent safety and hygiene laws, but there is no umbrella organization looking out for their interests as a group.

The government isn't paying them to stay in business. It's each bath for its own. But, in a country that just loves to get wet, business is booming. Which brings us to the third of Tokyo's "Super" Super Baths: this one a hot spring theme park called *Oedo-Onsen Monogatari*.

東京都公衆浴場業生活衛生同業組合

IV

UNDER THE BRIDGE

How hot springs enamored a pair
of seventh-century monarchs,
then the monkey shogun and finally the masses of old Edo

HAD WALT DISNEY BEEN Japanese, he probably would have dreamed up the Oedo-Onsen Monogatari. Or at least he would have really wished he had.

It's all so simple. Just as Americans love oversize stuffed mammals and thrilling rides, the Japanese love taking their clothes off and soaking with family and friends.

Eureka!

Wet n' Wild. N' Naked!

Well, all right. Maybe not quite *that* wild. After all, there are other places for that sort of thing, with a very different sort of infrastructure. What we are talking about here is good clean fun for the whole family. A bathing theme park. The kind of thing old Walt would have appreciated. And good business, to boot.

In retrospect, it was a no-brainer. Built to commemorate the 400th anniversary of Tokyo's supplanting Kyoto as the political center of Japan in 1603 (though it didn't really become the capital until 1868, when the Emperor decided to move in), the Oedo-Onsen Monogatari is a lovingly sentimental, and unabashedly inaccurate, reconstruction of a feudal neighborhood. The male employees—"cast members" to borrow the Disney term—sport topknot wigs and have fake samurai swords tucked into their sashes. The women wear their kimono after the fashions in vogue circa 1650, give or take a century or two.

Lest the effect be spoiled, even the guests are required to join in. When I made my first sojourn to the bath, for its gala grand opening, I was instructed along with several hundred other visitors to check my shoes at the gate, get a high-tech payment bracelet (though, fortunately, just about everything was on the house that day), and proceed to a counter where all prospective bathers choose a light, cotton yukata. The selection is one of the bath's bragging points; there are eighteen brightly colored designs, ranging from kabuki actors to Mount Fuji to the haunting faces of the tragic heroines of the pleasure quarters of yore.

This was, for me, almost painful. Standing at the counter, I was at a loss, which is unusual, especially since I was fully cognizant of the fact that before long it was all coming off anyway. Just the same, keenly aware of the crowds around me, I knew that this was a decision to take seriously.

I have a confession to make. Getting naked at a public bath isn't a problem. But no matter how I work the belt, tight and high or low and loose, yukata robes always seem to gradually pull open on me, especially if there is a lot of walking or sitting involved. Which is pretty much always. So I end up walking and sitting funny and exposing a lot more calf and cleavage than I'm comfortable with.

So, suddenly feeling as vulnerable as a little girl, I overcompensated by choosing a robe with the likeness of the biggest, fattest sumo wrestler you've ever seen. It didn't do me a whole lot of good. As I strutted out of the changing room, I felt not breezy, but drafty. At least I didn't have to don the top-knot toupee.

After selecting our wraparound apparel, we were herded to changing rooms and spat out into the Hirokoji central hall, a romantic re-creation of a seventeenth-century Tokyo locale, where there is a festive mood in the air and—thanks to a carefully painted ceiling and dimmed lights—the sun is always just beginning to set.

It isn't immediately apparent that this place has anything at all to do with bathing. The main hall, which is meant to resemble a neighborhood square, somehow has more of a goofy shopping mall ambiance to it. There are restaurants and beer stands. Fortunetellers sitting at little tables behind flickering lanterns read the palms of young couples, while children can throw ninja stars at red-and-white targets nearby. There are souvenir shops and stalls where sugar candy is spun and twisted and pinched into little birds or dragons or pandas. There's even a circus-style fish-for-prizes corner.

I, of course, had no time for any of it. I just wanted to get safely into the bath before my robe and I parted ways.

But it takes some navigating. Only after a short walk through feudal fantasyland does one arrive at the familiar doorway curtains with the curvy Japanese character ゆ for "yu," or hot water, hanging over the entrance to the baths.

Beyond them is yet another sprawling changing area. But, though bigger than most, the baths have a fairly conventional layout. Basically the same on the men's and women's sides—I know because I asked—the spa is centered around several indoor, tile-covered tubs, with both the traditional hot-and-deep variety and a more modern take on the Jacuzzi, in which bathers lie completely prone amid bubbly jets in shallow waters. There are waterfalls under which bathers stand, necks and shoulders exposed, to get a hydro-massage.

Through a set of sliding glass doors, there are rock-lined outdoor baths surrounded by more cascades and a well-coiffed garden. It is a surprisingly serene setting, but the impact of the intended slip back in time is somewhat muted by the taller buildings on the skyline and a crane or two at the nearby pier that poke up over the bath's outer fences. But what can you do? This is the heart of Tokyo, after all.

Like Disneyland—and Tokyo has one of those too—it's a very whole-some arrangement. There is no mixed bathing. Families or couples who want to enjoy the spa together have to settle for a winding stream-like "reflexology" footbath. And they do it with their yukata on.

Because it is only ankle-deep, guests need only tuck up the bottom of their robes before embarking on a little stroll over the stones embedded at the bottom (a rather painful experience, and judging from facial expres-sions, not only for me). The stream is designed to stimulate pressure points on the soles of the feet and thus promote a general feeling of well-being. But they promoted a more immediate feeling of rock-in-my-shoe syndrome, and I got out before any noticeable long-term benefits could be gained.

For extra fees, bathers can also have sand baths, mud baths, aromather-apy baths, massages. So many things to do. With or without the clothes on.

The spa's ads don't skimp on the obligatory claims of curative wonders. Bathers, they say, can find relief for neuralgia, muscle pain, painful joints, bursitis, paralysis of movement, stiff joints, bruises, sprains, chronic diges-tive problems, hemorrhoids, chills, lack of vigor, cuts, burns, chronic skin problems, chronic women's maladies and the aftermath of various illnesses. And they can help "feeble children." We wouldn't want to forget them.

Or the dogs. Once the success of the human baths was safely assured, the management opened up an annex, the Petite Dog Resort, where dogs can bathe in the same mineral waters, then have a relaxing shampoo, "moisturizing pack," or aromatherapy session. Or all of the above, for only ¥10,000 and up, depending on how big the pampered pet is.

"Here your dog can enter the bath as he or she pleases," a promotional blurb says. "Our trained staff can provide swimming therapy, trimming, and medical care. And only here can you buy your pet an original Edo-style yukata robe!" It probably goes without saying, but the canine resort has proven to be a huge hit.

Is it all a bit much? Well, yes. Of course. That's the idea.

The Oedo-Onsen Monogatari is totally over-the-top. It's camp. It's kitsch. But, like the acting in a Godzilla movie, it's a kick. In its own way, it works. This is almost certainly Japan's busiest hot springs facility, which means it is almost certainly the busiest in the world. Within just one year of its opening in a fashionable development along Tokyo's waterfront, the bath celebrated the arrival of its one-millionth visitor, which averages out to about 2,500 bathers each day (at about ¥2,000 a pop). On weekends and holidays, crowds cheerfully line up for waits of an hour or more to get in. At any given moment, the baths alone can hold a thousand bathers.

For purists, the spa—the name translates to "The Great Edo Hot Springs Tale"—was something of a fiction from the start. Mineral water doesn't conveniently bubble out of Tokyo's trendy Odaiba waterfront area. Developers had to drill almost a mile down and pump it out.

But that is totally missing the point. There's history in those waters.

THREE HOURS ON THE bullet train out of Tokyo, a short ride on the subway from the port city of Kobe, and another jaunt on a clunky local

express through a wooded hill scene, and we are now in Arima, which, the signs everywhere tell us, is the oldest hot springs resort in Japan.

For the ponderers out there, here's a logical dilemma. We could also be looking at signs saying that in Dogo, on the island of Shikoku. Or in the town of Shirahama. Or across the country and up in the mountains somewhere. Hot springs claiming to be the oldest in Japan are kind of like restaurants claiming to have the best chili in Texas, or England's best fish and chips.

Even so, the claim of venerability is usually not a complete scam. Stone tools and pottery shards found near a hot spring in Nagano, an inland province northwest of Tokyo, suggest prehistoric Japanese were using the waters for bathing and cooking at least six thousand years ago. Other evidence puts the use of hot springs in another Nagano site back as far as ten thousand years. Whenever, or wherever, the bathing began, there is no doubt that hot springs were a crucial aspect of daily life in many ancient villages well before the scattered population settled down into what could reasonably be called the Japanese nation.

And from about as early as there are records of Japan's imperial family, there are records of Japan's imperial family taking the waters. Arima was among their favorites.

Well over a millennium ago, the thirty-fourth emperor of Japan, Jomei, is said to have spent eighty-five days recuperating in the same rust-colored springs that I am now sharing with a gaggle of tourists at the *Kin no Yu*, or Golden Waters, a surprisingly nondescript, though pleasant enough, indoor bathhouse that is perhaps the most famous in Arima.

Jomei was such a devotee that he sought solace in Arima twice, in 631 and 638. What exactly he was hoping to cure is lost in the mists of time, but whatever it was, he apparently didn't exactly get a new lease on life after drying off. He died three years after his second visit.

Japan was a very different place back then. Especially when it came to the First Family.

On both his mother's *and* his father's side, Jomei was the grandson of Emperor Bidatsu, also known as Nunakurofutotamashiki. His mother, Princess Nukatehime, was the younger sister of his father, the Prince Oshisakahikohitonooe. Jomei was succeeded by Oshisakahikohitonooe's other son's daughter, Empress Kogyoku, who was thus Jomei's niece and also a great-granddaughter of Jomei's grandfather Bidatsu. To tangle the web even more, Kogyoku also became Jomei's wife, and they had three children. Their two boys—following in Mom and Dad's footsteps—went on to become emperors.

Like her husband, Kogyoku, who reigned twice, the second time under the name Saimei, was quite the hot springs fan. She visited Shirahama at least once, and in early 661, while preparing to mount an attack on the Korean kingdom of Silla, she set up a temporary capital in Ishiyu, where the Dogo spa is located. Before she could lead the troops into battle, however, she died.

Jomei may be the first known imperial bather, but he is certainly not the last. A steady stream of emperors and nobles, not to mention hundreds of thousands, if not millions, of commoners, followed him to this strangely secluded yet easily accessible hamlet. Emperor Go-Shirakawa came after he retired from the Chrysanthemum Throne in the late eleventh century, as did the retired Emperor Horikawa (1079–1107), just to name two. Underscoring the baths' firm position as a status symbol, Japan's notoriously esoteric aristocrats began writing poems about them (then again, they also gushed with praise over the various songs of bugs) from roughly the same time, starting a literary tradition that continues to this day, though it is no longer a product of the now-defunct nobility.

The famous court-life chroniclers Sei Shonagon and Murasaki Shikibu, two noble women who lived in the Heian Period (795–1192), also mentioned hot springs and bathing in their respective works, *The Pillow Book* and *The Tale of Genji*, which has been called the world's first novel. With typical whimsy, Sei Shonagon ranked people who don't bathe "even when the weather is hot" right up there with "rats' nests" and "children who sniffle as they walk" as one of the little annoyances in life that give an unclean feeling.

Like Arima, the hot springs of several other popular resorts are mentioned in Japan's first collection of poems, the *Manyoshu*, penned in the seventh and eighth centuries. Typically, the poem set in Yugawara, which isn't far from Tokyo, was more about the longings of a lonely lover than about the joys of mineral-laden fluids:

> Yugawara's seething springs
> Surge upward night and day
> Thus I yearn for my love's passion
> If she loves me or not
> My mind drifts astray.

Along with the monarchy, the fledgling clergy was also up to its neck in bathing from very early on in the game. In part because Buddha was said to have bathed his disciples, Buddhist temples became closely associated with hot springs, often taking on the responsibility of providing bathing facilities for the surrounding community. Today, Japan's oldest "public" bath can be found in Todai-ji, a temple in the ancient capital city of Nara that is famous for its huge sitting Buddha statue. They still have a metal tub there that dates back to 1197.

The importation of Buddhism to Japan from China via Korea in the sixth century brought new variety into the bath. Before long, three distinct types of bath had emerged: your basic hygienic baths for getting clean, healing baths, and baths with a more spiritual or social flavor. With the spread of monasteries, bathing evolved into a group endeavor and more often took place in large tubs or in steam rooms—or steam caves, as the case may be. The sponsorship of the elite fostered the growth of increasingly ostentatious bathing rituals or arrangements, and by the seventh century, it was all the rage for members of the ruling class to sponsor charity baths for the poor as a sort of alms.

When the warrior caste took over the government in the twelfth century, hot springs began to be frequently used by samurai in need of rest and recuperation. Minamoto no Yoritomo, Japan's first shogun, is said to have gone to Yugawara to heal a battle wound. He established his military capital in nearby Kamakura in 1192, and that same year sponsored a one hundred-day charity bath in memory of the recently departed Emperor Go-Shirakawa (the same one who visited Arima).

By the late medieval period, bathing hit its bubble years. Much of the credit goes to Toyotomi Hideyoshi, one of Japanese history's most colorful figures. A commoner born in a thatched hut to a poor farmer-warrior, who rose to become the nation's supreme general, Hideyoshi was an eccentric extraordinaire. He was also a shrewd strategist and an immensely talented social climber. He is credited with ending a century of civil wars and unifying Japan in 1582, only to then lead the country into a disastrous invasion of Korea on a campaign to conquer not just the peninsula itself but China as well.

After some initial successes, the war that began in 1592 stagnated for six years, until Hideyoshi's death. As the Japanese forces pulled out, they burned Seoul to the ground, the capping insult to a bitter campaign that

laid the foundations for the deep-seated animosity that continues to color relations between the two neighbors. A temple in Kyoto still has what is known as the *mimizuka*, a mound where the pickled noses and ears of 38,000 Korean civilians and soldiers were interred after being brought back from the campaign. Normally, the samurai would have brought back heads as their trophies, but there wasn't enough space on the ships home.

At any rate, Hideyoshi's final years were a boon for the arts and for cultured pursuits such as the bath and the tea ceremony. (Tea master Sen Rikyu was a Hideyoshi favorite, at least until they had a falling out and he was ordered to kill himself.) Often, Hideyoshi would combine the two, going on bathing excursions with his tea master, then throwing lavish bathing parties, with feasts and, in season, cherry blossom viewings.

Hideyoshi was the first military leader—because of his humble roots he was never made shogun, and instead used the title *taiko*, which is closer to prime minister—to build a bath in his castle. Completed in 1586 and demolished less than a decade later, his Jurakutei palace had a steambath, where he is believed to have held strategy meetings from time to time. His successors followed suit, making the bath a fixture in the palaces of the rich and powerful. Lesser nobles or samurai not able to afford the considerable cost of heating water took to holding bath gatherings, the equivalent of hot tub parties, at about this time. Instead of bringing their own bottles, each guest would share the cost of the bath.

Like Jomei, Hideyoshi was enamored with Arima. The year after becoming the most powerful man in the nation, he visited Arima on his first of many trips here. Over the years, he brought his wife and his consorts, and had flings with dozens of female bath attendants. After the great earthquake of 1597, he ordered a massive reconstruction of the village to protect its springs.

Hideyoshi saw other uses for the bath too.

Ishikawa Goemon was, by most accounts, a thief. His life remains a mystery; it has been the stuff of several kabuki plays (and many popular computer games) in which he is transformed into an outlaw of superhuman abilities—sometimes with Robin Hood-like tendencies—or a magnificent ninja.

But what really made Goemon immortal wasn't his life, but rather how Hideyoshi made him die. After breaking into the palace in an attempt to kill the ruler, Goemon was boiled in a cauldron of oil with his young son. To this day, cast iron tubs with the water heated from underneath are called *Goemon-buro*, or Goemon baths. Though not terribly popular, they have a solid niche market.

As for Hideyoshi, he never saw the completion of the Arima reconstruction. He died in 1598.

LET'S TAKE A STEP BACK, to put some of this in a global perspective. The year that the bath-loving Emperor Jomei died, 641, was the same year that Cairo was founded in Egypt and Chindaswinth defeated Tulga to become king of the Visogoths.

Okay, I had to look that up. But my point—that this bathing idea is an old one—is still valid. Even so, by the time of Jomei, bathing had in a very big way already come into—and gone out of—style in Europe.

Centuries before Christ, the ancient Greeks were displaying a special fondness for bathing. By the Homeric period they had built numerous bathing facilities, including one at Delphi, that they dedicated to their gods. Even Hippocrates, the man who gave us the Hippocratic Oath, was big on water.

To him, illnesses were the result of imbalances in the body fluids; he saw bathing as more than a way of getting clean. He theorized that bathing, perspiring, and exercise in general could help restore that balance, and before long a combination of the three became a common part of the Greek bathing regimen. The Greeks would exercise, bathe in circular baths, and then engage in philosophical discourse.

The Romans jettisoned most of that, instead coming up with some important twists of their own. Mainly, they put a bigger emphasis on the bath's relaxation value and its use as an R&R venue for soldiers. As the Empire spread out across Europe, the Romans established baths for their troops as far away as England (in Bath, of course) and Germany (Baden-Baden was originally a Roman spa), while their own *balnea publica* and *thermae* on the home front became increasingly lavish, sometimes large enough to hold several thousand bathers.

This was made possible by Rome's fabled aqueducts. In the first century A.D., 200 million gallons of water flowed through the aqueducts each day. The city had more than 920 public baths, and each citizen consumed an astonishing three hundred gallons of water daily (about four times the norm in most developed countries today).

Abandoning the austere Greek bent for mixing bath and exercise, the Romans turned their bathhouses into places for socializing, lounging, and the pursuit of hedonistic thrills. The hot water was believed to increase not only one's thirst, but the other appetites as well. Sex and debauchery took over until Hadrian, himself a thermae enthusiast, banned mixed bathing sometime between 117 and 138 A.D.

With the ascension of the early Christians after the fall of the Roman Empire in 476, bathing was doomed. Not only did the rise of Christianity in Europe usher in the Dark Ages, it also brought what could be called the Dirty and Smelly Ages. Bathing facilities were turned into churches, and the Christian propensity to see physical pleasures as evil (along with the still-fresh memories of Roman excesses) led to a bathing drought. For several centuries, bathing was decidedly out, and it wasn't uncommon for Europeans to abstain from the bath for months, or even years, at a time.

The influence of the Moors helped, at least partially, to change that from about the thirteenth century, when bathing was revived in southern Spain. Cordoba had several hundred bathhouses by that time. In Turkey and the Middle East, meanwhile, bathing in hamams remained a popular pastime. Baghdad is believed to have had 30,000 public baths at one point. Coming full circle, bathing made a solid rebound in Italy during the Renaissance, with scientific thinkers again trying to find the relationship between spring water and good health.

In 1473, the first printed work appeared on balneology. It was a compilation of essays on the waters of Porretta, a still-popular spa in Bologna. About a century later, another classic work on mineral waters, Andrea Bacci's *De Thermis Libri Septem*, treated bathing as a discipline worthy of study and, like pharmacology, complex enough to require the skills of a well-trained physician to properly administer. Arguing that taking the waters was not meant for the poor, Bacci opined that bathing wouldn't truly work as a cure unless it was accompanied by a quiet, comfortable lifestyle, and taken in a pleasant environment with lots of good food and wine.

But the tide of the times was flowing in the other direction. Dirty was, once again, the way to be.

From about the sixteenth until well into the nineteenth century, bathing was replaced by more limited washing practices, and perfumes and cosmetics were called in to cover up the stink and the mess. What baths did remain fell into disrepair and disrepute. The rise of the bubonic plague forced the closure of most by the end of the fourteenth century. Those that were left became little more than brothels. Like Hadrian before him, a scandalized

Henry VIII banned mixed bathing from his kingdom in 1546.

In 1547 Henry VIII died. But his edicts remained.

PROBABLY WITHOUT realizing it, the creators of the Oedo-Onsen Monogatari hot springs palace got one thing really right. The Edo Period was when bathing truly became a pleasure of the Japanese people. When it got crowded. And fun. And, at times, over the top.

After Tokugawa Ieyasu moved the seat of power from western Japan to Edo in 1603, the ruling elite found new baths to frequent. Their favorite hangouts—the seaside resort of Atami and Hakone, nestled away in the mountains—were both about sixty miles away. Kusatsu, another favorite, was a remote mountainous village twice the distance. So fond were they of getting wet that when they were unable to leave their castle, they had the water brought to them. Iemitsu, the third shogun in the Tokugawa era, was the first, ordering water from Atami.

It was not an easy order to fill. The trip from Hakone—which later became the shogun's main supplier—took two weeks, with each barrel carried by four men. The barrels were passed from shoulder to shoulder, and not allowed to touch ground until they were safely inside the castle's stone walls. Arduous though it was, the practice soon became a castle tradition, beginning in the mid 1600s and going strong for at least a century. Records show that from 1726 to 1734, some 3,642 barrels of hot-spring water were delivered to the castle. That's more than a barrel a day.

During the Edo Period, Japan's hot springs also got their first scientific examination. About seventy years before Italian physician Bacci got his ideas, Goto Konzan, a doctor in the capital, saw the benefits of bathing and tried to understand them in a systematic manner. His approach, however, was classical Chinese.

Konzan tried to explain the baths in terms of their impact on the body's *qi*, a kind of mystical force that is believed to flow through various meridians linked to the organs. The heart meridian, for example, runs down the arm and ends at the fingertips. Qi is the guiding principal behind acupuncture, with most of the points found along the meridian lines.

The Five Stagnations (of qi, blood, fluid, cold and food) were believed to be the cause of illness. Qi stagnation, for example, was thought to be the root of dizziness, hysteria, depression, and headaches. Konzan believed that hot spring bathing was therapeutic because it helped get qi flowing again.

But the real firsts, the ones that set the tone for today's bath culture, were taking place outside the castle, and beyond the society of the elite. The founding of the first public bathhouse in Edo in 1591 was followed by a bathhouse boom that brought public bathing to nearly every neighborhood. The ready availability fueled an interest in bathing that eventually sparked a travel industry based on the masses.

It started with a loophole. Despite his own humble origins, Hideyoshi had strengthened Japan's strict caste system, and the Tokugawa rulers were even more into controlling the common man. But while travel by commoners was subject to tight restrictions by the authorities, they did allow once-in-a-lifetime trips to places like the Grand Shrines of Ise—similar to the pilgrimages made by Muslims to Mecca. As the political stability created more economic opportunity and wealth in the non-ruling classes, the trips became wildly popular. In 1718 alone, more than five hundred thousand pilgrims made the trip to Ise. Another two hundred thousand trekked to Zenko-ji, a Buddhist temple in the mountains of Nagano, the city in the Japan Alps where the 1998 Winter Olympics were held.

But there was no rule saying the pilgrims couldn't stop along the way. It was, in fact, a necessity. Hot springs were almost always on the itinerary, and these pilgrimages created the foundations of what is today's domestic travel industry.

Back in the Edo days large groups were the rule. So was lots of communal drinking and singing and eating. Women were known to leave their husbands at home. Illustrated guidebooks detailing the minutia of each bath became bestsellers. Gimmicks were used to attract attention. Hot springs were even given rankings like sumo wrestlers. In one, Arima was deemed the ruler of the West, and Kusatsu the best of the East. It is uncanny how little has changed. All of the above could be said about the bath tourist industry of today, word for word.

And then there were the robes. It was in the Edo Period that the yukata, my nemesis, really came into its own. In the earlier days of bathing, when steambaths were more common, Japanese wore a thin white robe, called a *yukatabira* (*yu* means "hot water" and *katabira* means something like "undergarment"), into the bath to protect themselves from getting burned when they touched the walls. But when more people started actually getting into the water, the robe was donned before and after, and, since it was now being worn in a social context, it became more decorative.

So it was from the Edo Period that the yukata became a fixture at virtually every hot springs accommodation in the nation. Alas, the inescapable past.

V

HOT-SPRING FEVER

How food, flair and onsen-ism
draws the masses in numbers beyond measure.
Oh yes, and the baths.

I'M OUT OF THE BATH and I'm fully clothed. I'm sitting in front of multiple courses of an elaborate Japanese meal. I am here as a member of an international task force. The mission: To understand the true onsen experience.

We'd been immersed in an afternoon of bathing. But now it was all about the food. Hovering over me was Kaoru Ichikawa, proprietress of Kusatsu's Hotel Ichii. "I went twenty miles down the river this morning to collect those maple leaves," she says, flashing a nervous yet proud smile as she points to a garnish that has just been distributed with a dish about midway through our dinner. "I wanted everything to be perfect."

She had reason to be expectant. "Lavish" is one of those words that, unless you move in unusually well-to-do circles, you rarely use. But on this evening, she had just defined for me the meaning of "lavish." It was perhaps the best meal I have ever had.

It began with rice wine, a dry, obscure local concoction, which was in itself a fine touch. But it was served with gold flakes dancing in the bottom of our tiny, frosted glasses. *Real* gold. And the golden saké flowed freely for the next three hours.

The first course, prepared by grand chef Shigeyuki Kuroiwa, who made a cameo appearance after dessert and was roundly applauded, was shrimp cocktail and a tofu-like sesame paste, followed by boiled crab legs, and duck with scallops. A plate of nouveau sushi. Prosciutto, with mozzarella cheese and cherry tomatoes and basil sauce. A boiling stew with a delicate *dashi* broth. Raw tuna, salmon, and sweet lobster sashimi. Boiled and seasoned turnips, taro and whitefish. *Chawanmushi*, featuring a touch of sea urchin and slices of fragrant *matsutake* mushrooms. Grilled and salted fish, with a splash of lime. A cut of beef steak, with sides of potatoes, mushrooms, zucchini, and white asparagus. Fried, mashed shrimp, with more mushrooms and hot peppers. Noodles, with *wasabi*. Various kinds of pickles in the hues of autumn. Vegetable soup. Vanilla ice cream. Papaya slices. Melon. Strawberries. Persimmons, grown in the garden outside. Hot green tea. Or more gold flake-laden sake.

The parade of plates, brought to us by a team of silent young women in blue and pink kimono, was as carefully choreographed as a Broadway musical. Beautiful menus—in hand-drawn calligraphy—placed beside each guest's black-and-red lacquered table detailed every offering in the thirteen courses that comprised this magnificently devised dinner.

The courses were carefully listed under categories that ranged from the internationally familiar—"raw," for example, is sashimi, and usually comes early in the meal—to the more esoteric. The pickles, often yellow, fall under *konomono*, and come toward the end. Though a couple more steps removed from the river than sashimi, *yakimono*, the fried fish dish, is judged by how much life and vigor the presentation suggests. Even a mediocre meal must have a fish—always served whole, with scales and eyes still intact—that appears ready to jump off the plate. Ours were captured before us in mid-arch, seemingly oblivious to their recent defeat by the fisherman's hook, a slice of lime and ginger offering a hint of color.

It is all very seasonal. And visual. Each dish is a vignette, an intimation of the continuum of life, and displayed on an array of fine tableware that, even without any food on it, could whet the appetite of the most discerning aesthete.

I have another confession to make (besides being yukata challenged): I'm not even really all that much of a fan of Japanese cuisine. Being an American at heart, I like my food hearty. I've often thought that serious Japanese food is primarily a feast for the eyes; the taste only secondary. I suppose that, when well done, it can work both ways. And, every so often, I honestly do wish I could have seconds of something. But fixing up a real belly-satisfying meal doesn't seem to be the goal of most self-respecting Japanese chefs.

In Japan, the final judgment of a good meal isn't left to the taste of the beholder. Or, should I say, the whims of the tongue must at times be vetoed by the more transcendental appreciations of the mind. It's like haiku. You have to understand your seasonal cues. You have to know your limitations, your rules and conventions. Even to call it cooking is kind of off track, since a lot of it isn't cooked to begin with. It's prepared, planned out, displayed, replete with lots of little subplots and nuanced phrases.

Food is just one aspect of the art of eating. Mrs. Ichikawa, our hostess, was not only trying to feed us. She was plucking us from our lives and depositing us smack-dab in the ceremony of the feast.

We were given special party coats to wear. There was a display of ikebana, with four-foot-tall sprigs of pine intermeshed with sparkling ornaments of gold and silver, big enough for children to hide in at the center of the sprawling, tatami mat-covered banquet hall she had chosen for us. There was traditional dancing by a local geisha sextet and a troupe of bare-legged drummers, pounding away as the night drew to its climax.

Petite but dynamic and self-confident, Mrs. Ichikawa, who has run the Hotel Ichii since the death of her husband, was herself a delicate presentation. She had been coiffed for the night. Her makeup was perfect. Her kimono, silvery gray with a tasteful blue sash, was sublime. And over each guest she hovered, like a butterfly seeking the nectar of appreciation she so certainly deserved.

By the end of the party, everyone was sated. Many of us were drunk and feeling jolly. After a short bus ride to our own inn, a larger facility on the other side of town, we would be naked again in the natural heat of our hostess' little corner of Japan. It was a fine day for the senses.

"You know, this is what hot springs culture is really all about," she had said after a few minutes at my table discussing the finer points of the meal. "It's a party culture. It's a social affair. It's about pleasure."

BUT THE TRIP WASN'T just about having fun.

I had arrived in Kusatsu by bus from Tokyo early that day at the invitation of the city government. As soon as I got there, officials loaded me and a dozen or so other foreigners they had brought up for the weekend into a van for a drive around town. We were then deposited at Kusatsu's steaming outdoor bath, big enough to pass for a small lake, where we proceeded to strip down and test the waters.

Kusatsu officials had come to the conclusion that the whole hot springs phenomenon just wasn't appreciated well enough outside of Japan. They had decided this was a real problem and had turned it into something of a crisis. So they hastily arranged this international symposium to urgently increase awareness and, hopefully, spread the word. They even had a specific word in mind—"Onsen-ism."

The rationale went like this: "Hot springs," which is how "onsen" is normally translated into English, doesn't quite capture the true meaning of what hot spring culture in Japan really encompasses. Onsen-ism, they said, signifies not just the bath, but the whole experience that goes with it, from the inn where you stay to the food that you eat. The bathing life.

While not getting a whole lot of press elsewhere in Japan, this matter of semantics was steaming up a lot of collars in the barber shops and community centers of Kusatsu, where just about everybody's livelihood flows in one form or another from the 9,500 gallons of water that gush up from below their town each minute.

So Kusatsu, a mountainous, snowy burg of several thousand in the landlocked province of Gunma, had decided that it was time for the rest of the world to wise up and start using the word "onsen." "What we want is for it to become a word like 'geisha' or 'kimono,' something that everybody everywhere recognizes immediately, something that immediately conjures up an image," Eiichi Ichikawa, a gray-haired, snaggle-toothed official in charge of Kusatsu's "planning and creation division," told me soon after I got into town. "We just don't think 'hot springs' really conveys what this whole culture is all about. We think this is a huge disappointment."

Like all tourism officials in Kusatsu that wintry weekend, Ichikawa (no relation to the Hotel Ichii proprietress) wore over his business suit a *happi* coat with the word "Onsen-ism" written in big black letters across his back. It wasn't only about Kusatsu, he said. The real problem was with Japan's image.

People overseas just aren't interested in coming here, he lamented. At

least, not as tourists. Businesspeople will come if necessary, but foreigners on vacation just aren't thinking Japan. They go to sightsee in China. They go hiking in Nepal. Shopping in Hong Kong, dining in Singapore. But they stay away from Japan.

A few years ago, a phrase had even been coined in frustration over the situation—"Japan passing," as in Japan being passed over. It was considered far worse than the coinage it was meant to resemble, "Japan bashing," which denoted the anger directed at Japan at the height of the trade wars with the United States in the 1980s.

I was familiar with this argument. Places like the Golden Pavilion in Kyoto and, of course, Mount Fuji, have a certain caché internationally. Tokyo has its own weird sort of big-city charm, but nothing like, say, Paris. And while there are plenty of good beaches in Japan, who would come all the way here to lie on one, when they could go to a sun-drenched resort in Thailand, or a secluded island in the Philippines?

Personally, I've always seen this as being the result of one obvious drawback. Money. Doing just about anything in Japan costs two arms and a leg. Getting to Kusatsu by bus that day had cost me about forty dollars, one way. A quick coffee at the bus station cost me three dollars more. Unless you go solo and on the cheap, weekend trips to hot springs can easily run up to the thousand dollar mark. And still, in all my time here, I have never heard any good solutions to the cost issue. It's just taken for granted.

Still, fears over the tourist glut prompted Tokyo to put together the Visit Japan Campaign, a government-backed advertising blitz with the express goal of bringing in an annual ten million tourists by 2010, double the number of when the campaign began in 2002. So far, the campaign has had only modest results. Visitors to Japan still pay exorbitantly high prices for their hotel rooms and dinners, but at the main airports those who do come are now treated to recorded messages from the prime minister himself, touting the wonders of the country they are about to see. Which doesn't seem like the most effective advertising, since I presume everybody at the airport is already sold on the idea of coming.

But up in the mountains of Gunma, such skepticism was out of season. Officialdom at the highest levels of the national government had decided this country has a tourism problem. And since tourism in Japan has always meant hot springs first and foremost, officials in Kusatsu were doing their part as good Japanese by putting their heads together and trying to figure out how they could help. The symposium was the answer, partly sponsored by the Japanese government as one facet of the Visit Japan Campaign.

Kusatsu wasn't itself in any particular danger. Nearly 6,000 people overnight here everyday, and another 3,400 visit on day trips. That adds up to 3.4 million tourists a year, which is not bad for a town of only 7,000 people. The number of visitors has been roughly the same for more than a decade, with a marginal increase in day-trippers. Best of all, the overnighters tend to include a high percentage of tourists who have been to Kusatsu before and are likely to come again.

At the height of the winter season, Kusatsu's main street is quite a sight. Tourists swarm in by the busload, spending large sums of money before leaving. The town remains eerily empty while they fill the ski slopes by day and the baths by night. But, in between, right around dinnertime, they come out in droves, wandering around, checking out the local sights and keeping the dozens of souvenir shops that line the main avenue doing a brisk business. There are specialty shops selling everything from gourmet pickles to fancy knives. Mostly, though, it's just trinkets. Key chains, mugs, knickknacks.

Breaking away from the official entourage for a moment, I pop into a

xviii

crowded sweet shop where shelves are covered with neat rows of *manju*, a popular delicacy found all over the country. At hot springs resorts, the manju—bite-sized buns filled with sugary bean-paste—are steamed in the vapors of the local mineral waters. Like everyone else visiting that day, I buy a couple dozen of the buns to take back to my colleagues in Tokyo—a Japanese custom that keeps many a souvenir shop in business.

Since I'm there on the taxpayers' dime, the village has put me up in a relatively cheap Western-style hotel. But it's still an impressive facility, with its own golf course, hiking trail, indoor pool, bowling alley and rooms that range in price from ¥10,000 to ¥20,000 a night, per head. Elsewhere, in the good inns, prices basically begin at around that price and head off skyward from there. One of my favorite hot springs starts at ¥50,000, or ¥100,000 a night for a couple.

Of course, we're talking about a scroll hanging in the alcove, a vase with a delicate flower arrangement, the soft scent of incense, a hot pot of tea awaiting you as a maid spreads your futon on the tatami. A view of the garden. A room that could comfortably sleep five or ten people. Two very impressive meals included.

I've only gone once. And I stayed just one night. But even if I could afford it, I probably couldn't go often. The place is always booked solid several months in advance, generally by regulars. Wealthy regulars.

Though Kusatsu itself is in good shape, there are some worrisome trends. According to one of the symposium's guest speakers—Junji Yamamura, a hot springs specialist at Chiba University (yes, hot springs studies is a valid major at many Japanese universities)—the market is rife with problems.

For one thing, he said, it's oversaturated. In 2002, some 137 million people stayed overnight at hot springs in Japan. That amazing number includes quite a few "repeaters"—there are only about 120 million Japanese. This

overnighter statistic has stayed relatively flat over the years, as has the number of hot springs— 3,000 of them—with overnight facilities.

But here's the problem—the number of those facilities at the hot springs—
the inns and bathhouses and spas—has more than doubled since 1965, to
nearly 30,000. There aren't more hot springs resorts, and there isn't even very
much more water coming out of the ground. It's just being used by a whole
lot more places with baths. And probably by a lot more day-trippers, though
that statistic is hard to pin down.

Yamamura noted that from 1954 to 1978 there was a huge, continuous
swell in the hot springs business in Beppu, another of the country's premiere
resort towns. But after a relatively long stretch of prosperity, that is beginning to shrink again. He also noted the sinking fortunes of Atami—which
saw great growth in the 1970s. The seaside resort—once the favorite of the
shoguns and later a popular gathering place for Japan's gangsters—has now
fallen on hard times.

Part of the reason for the overheated growth was politics. Seeing the
mushrooming of the hot springs industry, and a chance to lock up votes in
the construction and tourism sectors, Noboru Takeshita, selected as Japan's
prime minister in 1987, came up with a policy initiative ostensibly aimed at
reinvigorating the country's small towns by giving them all ¥100 million to
spend as they pleased.

Panned by economists as an utter waste of a huge amount of taxpayer
money, the program was one of the last great examples of the old-style pork-
barrel politics that had kept Takeshita's conservative party, ironically called
the Liberal Democrats, in power for virtually all of the post-World War II era.
The Liberal Democrats had always been the party of construction, of high-
ways and bridges, needed or not, and too lazy or distracted to come up with
any more-specific projects, they were now basically just handing out checks.

In the end, the scheme didn't much help Takeshita—he and most of the rest of the party's leadership were forced to resign because of an influence-peddling scandal in 1989. His brief tenure did, however, leave a deep impression on the hot springs industry.

SEVERAL HUNDRED OF the 3,300 towns that benefited from the government's largesse spent their money drilling holes from which they planned to pump out a new life for themselves. Within a few years, there were hot springs all over the place.

But at about the same time, an economic slowdown hit, then settled in to stay for well over a decade. The towns that had bought into the hot springs industry now found that there was more competition for fewer bathers, and funding for the upkeep of their wells started to run dry. On the private front, the intensified competition was also too intense to sustain, making more baths go belly-up, especially in overextended resort areas like Atami that jumped too quickly at the less-devoted, more gimmick-oriented bather.

"What that all did was underscore the need for hot springs resorts to develop their image as a unique locality, not a copy of what can already be found in the city, if they are going to compete," Yamamura said. "The best hot springs have already done this, and it is proving to be very good business."

Kusatsu is a model of the local-flair approach. It is a small town through and through. After dark, it closes down. Among the main souvenirs to be had here are eggs boiled in hot springs water, and a type of dumpling that might well have been eaten by farmers in the feudal days. The high point of the daily entertainment schedule involves a bunch of old women smacking a tub of water with wooden paddles, a throwback to the days when the hot spring water had to be stirred up to cool it down for bathers to use.

But Kusatsu is a microcosm of Japan in that, while the Japanese themselves love Kusatsu, foreigners are staying away. According to Ichikawa, only about 10,000 non-Japanese, virtually all of them Asians, make their way to Kusatsu in an average year. If foreigners were to come to Kusatsu in the same kind of numbers that Japanese do, the thinking goes, there would be 125,000 "international" bathers visiting each year, a tenfold increase. "We really see this as our growth market," Ichikawa told me.

So, in the name of national crisis, for the next two days Kusatsu delved into its series of lectures, slide shows, and studies by foreign and Japanese experts aimed at figuring out how to make that growth market grow. Though earnest, it was a naive, almost sad exercise. On the second morning, we were shown a promotional video featuring a blond American girl in a brightly colored yukata robe explaining Kusatsu's attractions for a foreign audience. She spoke in English. But, for a reason no one seemed to be able to make sense of, her voice was drowned out by that of the Japanese narrator, who spoke in broken English.

MORE THAN JUST about any other hot springs resort in Japan, Kusatsu owes its fame to a foreigner. After the fall of the feudal Tokugawa government in 1868, Japan's reformist rulers realized that if they were to keep the country from being reduced to a colony by the Western powers, they had to lead it down the road to modernization, and they had to act quickly. In an inspired policy, they decided to invite hundreds of foreign experts to bring the country up to speed in virtually every field—Prussians were imported to teach law and the tactics of modern warfare, British civil engineers were brought in, American educators filled the schools.

Soon, Japan had its first trains and lighthouses, gas lamps and breweries, race tracks and bakeries. It had a modern, Western-style constitution by the turn of the century, and students of science at the prestigious University of Tokyo were learning Darwin's newfangled theory of evolution.

The lessons didn't come cheap. By 1874, when their numbers reached 520, the combined salaries of the foreign experts accounted for roughly one-third of Japan's annual budget. Doctor Erwin von Baeltz, a native of the southern German town of Bietigheim-Bissingen, arrived in Japan at the age of twenty-seven to teach medicine at the University of Tokyo in June 1876. Though most of the experts left after a year or two, Baeltz made Japan his life. He married a Japanese woman, and the couple raised their children here. His first tour lasted through the end of July 1892, and he returned the following year for another stay that lasted until 1902, well after the Japanese government had officially abandoned its foreign expert program.

Like many of the foreigners, Baeltz's impact was deep and wide. Baeltz was a strong believer in the importance of sport, and one of his protégés at the University of Tokyo, Jigoro Kano, later became the founder of modern judo. Baeltz even marketed a popular medicine called "Baeltz water," which was used for the treatment of skin ailments. But the German doctor's most lasting contribution may have been his advocacy of Japanese hot springs, which he believed to have tremendous healing powers and which he wrote about extensively.

Kusatsu, being relatively accessible to Tokyo, was one of his favorites. Just two years after his arrival in Japan, he made the first of many journeys to the small town, and in his writings he described it as a symbol of Japan's hot springs culture. For bringing the town a measure of international fame, he now has the honor of a Baeltz Museum and a Baeltz Street. A bronze statue of Baeltz stands in the Kusatsu town square.

But the Kusatsu of Baeltz's time wasn't a very happy place. It was, instead, a hard-core sanatorium, where the sick endured an almost torturous regime

in their effort to get well. Beginning soon after dawn, and repeated at three-hour intervals, a loud alarm would blast, informing the legions of the ill in Kusatsu that it was time to gather at the town's main bath. Wearing cotton robes and sandals, the bathers would swarm out of their inns and teahouses and make their way to the *netsu-no-yu* (or fever bath), or other similar facilities near a steaming bayou of sharp-smelling, yellowish-green sulfuric acid that is located at the center of town.

At this point, the water-beating ritual would begin, with loud shouting and pounding as groups of townspeople used their wooden planks to agitate and cool the waters from their natural state of about 130°F—well beyond the comfort zone of any human. At the order of the chief attendant, all bathers would begin dipping out ladles of the scalding water and dousing it over their heads and shoulders to prepare themselves for the bath ahead.

A "ready" was called out. The bathers responded, probably with a good measure of trepidation. Then all jumped in in unison and remained, if they could endure it, for exactly three minutes, about as long as their skin, brains, and hearts could make it without suffering serious damage. The attendant would call out after one minute, then two, then two and a half, and then he would count down the final fifteen seconds. The bathers would emerge sweating profusely, their skin bright red. The prospect of repeating the ritual throughout the day was undoubtedly not a pleasant one.

But they were not there for fun. These baths were full of the ill seeking a cure, and the mood was dark, depressed. There was no merrymaking, no small talk. And to make bathing here even more of an ordeal, the waters were, and remain, highly acidic. I had trouble sleeping after my first day because my eyes would burn every time I tried to shut them.

Baeltz was, nonetheless, a fan of Kusatsu and swore by its health benefits, saying it was good for rheumatic ailments, gout, eye diseases and a malady similar to beri beri. Even lepers had their own bath at Kusatsu. But Baeltz's contemporary, Henry Spencer Palmer, the *Times* correspondent who wrote so glowingly of the nearby town of Ikaho, had a less forgiving view. Palmer, after a visit in 1886, described Kusatsu as "purgatory," a "dull hollow without prospect."

It was, he said, a place populated by "an ailing, woebegone, and joyless crowd, almost wholly of the lower orders who seek, by painful processes to get rid of maladies which in many cases are of the most frightful kind, and who have no more cheerful occupation than that of watching their own symptoms as the days and weeks go wearily by." Bathing at Kusatsu, he concluded, "is a solemn and bitter penance, submitted to at stated hours and under medical advice."

THIS FACE OF BATHING in Japan has vanished. Though the old and the infirm still seek the cure of the waters, only a very rare few are willing to do so without the comforts of a nice inn, good food, and the company of friends or lovers.

Even back in the times when a visit to Kusatsu was like a prolonged visit to the dentist, the role of the bath as a hedonistic escape was well established. In the feudal era, hot springs were popular enough to have spawned their own literature. There were travel books and woodblock prints gushing over their pleasures, with their medicinal powers relegated to the back seat. It was good fun. It was a vacation, and the guides were written accordingly. One of the seventeenth-century hot spring ranking sheets that mimicked the sumo rankings decorates a wall at Kusatsu's hot springs museum. Despite its dark reputation, Kusatsu is at the top of the list, with the sumo-derived rank of *ozeki*, or champion. The list was, after all, written by a Kusatsu native.

Marking a direct descent from these guides of old, there continues to be a hugely popular genre of travel literature devoted to hot springs. Monthly magazines and seasonal guidebooks have their own section in most bookstores—usually right up front. Women's magazines run features on them constantly, emphasizing their healing properties and highlighting their dinner menu. Just for the hell of it, I did a quick check of five racy weekly men's magazines the other day, and all five had pictures of semi-naked women in hot spring baths.

But television is the real media for hot springs. In season—mainly the fall and winter—it seems almost every program features actors and actresses cavorting around in their bath towels, ecstatically taking the waters and then relaxing at an inn and gushing over how wonderful the food is. There are even game shows featuring onsen.

It's perfect for TV—suggestive, yet not outright naughty. Censors and sponsors go for that. Showing babes wrapped up in bath towels daintily wading into the bath and sitting down, leaving their bare shoulders and necks exposed, gets Dad's attention, yet violates no broadcast regulations. And Mom wants to go because it looks so relaxing.

Throwing in a comedian or two and getting the young ladies to play all kinds of silly games, thus showing more legs and necks, is a natural progression. Plus, the hot springs are willing to foot much of the cost, since it's all publicity.

Even so, I'm partial to the books—of which there are more than two hundred in print. On my desk are two popular guides, whose titles translate as: "The Great Satisfaction Guide to Hot Springs and Inns in the Kanto Region" and the weekly "Famous Hot Springs of Japan." Between the two, I would guess some five hundred inns and baths are duly introduced.

It's a very dry business. The baths being introduced are almost always depicted in the same manner, with a photo or two of the bathing areas (indoor and outdoor whenever possible, and either completely empty or with a pretty girl politely covered by a well-placed towel), a photo of the rooms, and a photo or two of the meals (always big and colorful). This is followed by a written description of whatever is in the waters, how many rooms are available at the inn, how much they cost, phone numbers, Web sites, how to make reservations.

The layout says a lot. The waters are just one element of the whole bathing package, and—as Hotel Ichii proprietress Ichikawa suggested, and I experienced—they are, in the minds of many, not even the most important element. Just getting wet isn't enough. The industry has evolved into a much more varied pursuit of pleasure. It is the closest thing the normally stoic Japanese have to socially sanctioned hedonism.

Bathing resorts provide the delights of the water, plus gourmet delights and—this is important—a private, discrete and comfortable getaway where couples can partake of each other's sensual delights après the bath. It would be hard to imagine onsen-ism any other way. What with all the nudity and the focus on sensual pleasures, there is a strong though unspoken undertone of sex at hot springs resorts. Many inns won't even accept unaccompanied singles.

The first time I visited a hot springs resort to report on the water-tainting scandal, I asked several young and middle-aged couples for their opinions. Then, in keeping with normal journalistic practice, I asked for their names—a question that was met with expressions of horror. To my surprise, roughly a quarter of the couples I approached were rather obviously there on the sly.

In a sense, the great effort made to tout the medicinal value of bathing is something of a smoke screen. If the Japanese bathing masses were really out for a cure, they would bathe the way they used to bathe in Kusatsu. There

諸國温泉鑑見

大坂

would be doctors on hand, as there are at European spas, and the bathers would be sick with something more specific than the simple wear and tear of day-to-day life.

But the Japanese are very Calvinistic. To be acceptable, the cultivation of pleasure must involve a deeper purpose, it must be couched, for example, in the pursuit of a philosophy, of a deeper understanding of life. Or of the cure to an ill. Because the baths have that curative element, bathers need not feel guilty that they are just frivolously eating, drinking, and being merry. They are working on their health situation. It's a self-improvement thing.

And that's not only acceptable, it's a social duty.

BACK AT THE DINNER party, Mayor Takashi Nakazawa and Yamamura, the hot springs professor, had joined Mrs. Ichikawa at my table and were waxing philosophical about onsen-ism.

Yamamura said he felt that, along with satisfying the pleasure principle, hot springs serve a more noble role in modern Japanese society, in that they provide the nation with a place to—excuse the pun—let off steam. "They are like stress-relief clinics," he said. "The Japanese really need these facilities to keep their sanity."

This was something of a kicker to his gloomy lecture earlier on the threat of how the industry could well soon find itself on the verge of disaster—like their urban cousins, the public baths. An increasing number of hot springs are already falling prey to the caprice of the changing economy, he warned.

"Twenty years ago, people would have laughed at me if I said this industry is in trouble," he said. "Now they are listening when I say we have to come up with a new paradigm."

The mayor, however, seemed unconcerned. A fashionably dressed man with a buzzcut and a face full of closely cropped salt-and-pepper whiskers,

Nakazawa was born and raised in Kusatsu. He has the sophisticated air of one who has enjoyed the benefits of a good education and has spent enough time abroad to appreciate that there are a multitude of interesting and perhaps even valid takes on what life might be all about, and that not all of them require long, repeated dips in the steaming hot water of Kusatsu.

As he listened politely to Yamamura, he seemed to be strangely unconcerned about the business side of bathing. And he didn't seem very interested in looking for a new paradigm. His idea of onsen-ism was pretty straightforward. "It's a way of life," he said, emptying a beer and chewing on a toothpick. "It's our way of life."

VI

NAKED ENCOUNTERS

The whole mixed bathing thing.
The importance of knowing how to wield a towel,
and when to drop the trunks.
The bans, the returns, the switch to swimsuits.
Why getting naked together is getting hard

IT'S CROWDED IN the bath today. I am surrounded by people. But perhaps because they are strangers, and perhaps because they are naked, they register more as a collection of their parts, creating the strong—and deeply disconcerting—impression that I am embedded in a landscape of butt cracks, male nipples, distended bellies, swinging scrota.

Because I wanted to be able see my way around the bathing area, which is large and slippery, I wore my glasses—a decision I now regret. Despite the occasional burst of blur from the steam rising up around me, I can see everything with crystal clarity. Everything.

It's okay, I tell myself. This is a bath. Nudity is normal here. Totally normal, I tell myself. Over and over.

I'm not the squeamish type. Never have been. I once saw a dead body floating upside down in the churning waters off the island of Okushiri which had just been devastated by a horrible tsunami. Its torso weighted down by some unseen anchor, the corpse floated by our Coast Guard cutter with its boots sticking up. Because of the motion of the water, it appeared to be walking, flipped over, briskly trotting by. I was going in on the ship with the first squad of out-of-town riot police mobilized to help with the rescue efforts, and a young officer next to me held his mouth and gagged as the body went silently passed us.

I was pretty much okay with that. This, however, is creeping me out. When, I'm thinking, did the human race go to seed? Are naked males completely void of any kind of aesthetic value? And hold on. Wait. Do I look like that too?

My glasses frustratingly impervious to the steam, I close my eyes and lean back my head, trying to concentrate on the pleasant warmth of the water. No use. The images are right there, thrown into even bolder relief by the blackness of the back of my eyelids. I try to conjure up something sublime to ground my thoughts. I seek refuge in the wisdom of Auguste Rodin. Surely the artist who created The Thinker, a celebration of Man and his transcendental beauty, must have some solace for me right now.

"Man's naked form belongs to no particular moment in history," Rodin once said. "It is eternal, and can be looked upon with joy by the people of all ages."

Nice try.

At this particular moment the naked thigh of a man who has just climbed in next to me rubs up against my own. "*Sumimasen*," he says with a little smile, sweat and bathwater dripping down his flushed face. The only thing Rodin got right about my encounter with this Everyman was that the moment does seem to last an eternity.

My protective bubble has just been popped. I try to focus again. I am here for a reason. I remind myself that it's actually good that there is such a crowd in the bath. The perfect environment for me to conduct my little experiment. Well, actually, that's a little presumptuous. It's really more of a comparison.

I'M AT A PLACE CALLED Yunessun, deep in the mountains of Hakone. Just a couple hours' drive south of Tokyo, Hakone, austere and visibly volcanic, has for centuries been one of the premiere bathing areas in all of Japan. Some of the best of the older-style inns are to be found here, with all the pleasures of good food and fine lodgings that the venerable bathing tradition has to offer. There is even a Hakone Geisha Association. But I deliberately took a pass on that today.

Yunessun is brand-new. Unlike the grander, more historically suggestive names of its neighbors, Yunessun isn't even written in Chinese characters (which is always a sign of newness). I believe it's a pun, since *yu* means hot water, and *netsu* means heat. Or maybe it has some obscure meaning in German.

What drew me to this particular bathers' paradise is the fact that it is perhaps the nation's most comprehensive, ambitious attempt to give the people—all the people—what they want.

In the brochures, this place looked awesome. Yunessun has Turkish style hamams: it has pools in the ancient Roman design. There's a bath with blue, minty-smelling water that is set in front of a giant tank of bobbing, frilly jellyfish supplied by a local aquarium. I found this one very soothing, though a woman next to me said it stank of dishwasher liquid and got out after a couple of minutes. There's a section called "Yutopia" (see, the owners really *do* like their puns) with a bath set under a huge tea pot that pours out green tea, and another under a gushing keg of sake. There's one with red wine, another splashing over with coffee. Twenty-five different baths in all.

Salvador Dali—or Aldous Huxley during his "The Doors of Perception" phase—would have felt right at home. But what I found most interesting was how the layout of Yunessun, with all of its varied water zones, so perfectly encapsulates the modern Japanese take on the proper way to handle the issue of public nudity. Basically, they cubbyhole.

The bathing park is divided into nude and swimsuit zones, and the nude zone is divided into a men's side and a women's side. There is no naked mixing. Contrary to many of the stereotypes out there, that's pretty much how it goes these days. But what I couldn't figure out was why there was a nude zone at all. All things considered, and with the tide of modern modesty flowing away from the open flaunt—in this country at least, but we'll get back to that—it seemed like a valid question.

As I sat naked and recoiled from the overload of alien skin bombarding my senses, the answer seemed anything but obvious. Having nothing but other men to look at certainly took most of the thrill out of being naked, for me anyway. And I'm sure that feeling was shared by my fellow bathers. This was clearly not a gay hangout. So the reason wasn't sexual. But once the sexual part is eliminated, what's left? Ambiance?

The naked zone was quite nicely set up. After disrobing, bathers walk out to a stone-lined bath that is indoors, but airy. One wall is taken up by glass, part of which slides open, providing both a clear view of the wooded grounds beyond and access to the stairs that lead to them. For those who choose to remain indoors, there is a sauna and another large communal tub, this one made of wood and with an equally impressive view outdoors.

The area, called *Mori no Yu*, or the Hot Water Woods, is filled with pine trees, shrubbery, and rugged rockscapes. Water sprays softly across the outdoor stairs to keep them warm and free of ice. There is a faint smell of sulfur in the air, suggesting that this part of the complex is an active hot springs, or at least fed by one. Over the bamboo fences that mark the edge of the bathing area, the forested hills of Hakone fill the rugged horizon. It is peaceful and natural, albeit in a naggingly contrived, manmade way.

My mind connects a couple of dots here. Something about the natural motif requires nudity. Or perhaps the natural motif is enhanced by nudity. The two do go hand in hand.

The swimsuit zone, with all its amusement park gimmicks, makes no attempt at pretending to be a return to nature. After all, bathing naked in a tub full of coffee, or rice wine, would seem almost unsanitary (though, truth is, the baths are mostly just colored water). With many others, I floated face-up in the Dead Sea bath, so salty a scrape on my ankle stung. That would certainly have been a very different experience naked.

THERE IS A CERTAIN LINE that must be crossed to go around naked in front of others, especially strangers. Other than when we are bathing, we normally don't get naked. Some people may sleep in the nude, or every now and then lounge around their apartments in the nude, but in our adult, everyday lives nudity is a pretty alien concept. Even when we are just by ourselves, and free to expose whatever we please with no fear of it being looked on askance by anyone, most of us choose not to. It's not even a choice, really. Being clothed is, ironically, usually more natural than being naked.

Breaking with the clothing rule in public is even more iffy. I mean, when do we ever really do that? For many, never. Maybe when we were kids, changing after P.E. or school sports. Or, as adults, for a shower at the gym following a workout. There are times—usually uncomfortable—when we may be asked to get naked in front of a doctor or a nurse. Or a masseuse. Otherwise, nudity usually involves sex.

But does it have to be that way? Being something of a country boy, I've been skinny dipping more than a few times. My initiation was at a lake fed by a glacier so far back in the Tatoosh Mountains of Washington State that I would have had to be hopelessly paranoid to even entertain the thought of anyone other than my hiking partner seeing me there. Besides, I was sweaty, and dirty. I needed the bath. It was a very pragmatic matter.

But it still felt a little thrilling. The water was freezing. The mountain air was bracing. And I was naked. Out in the wild. I had never felt quite like that before. It was a rebellious moment of freedom, but somehow a shy, quiet one.

The second time, I was with several friends on a boat. It was a beautiful summer evening, with the sun just beginning to set on a calm, inviting blue sea. We were all feeling good and, for various reasons, our inhibitions were down. So we stripped off our clothes and jumped in. No hesitation. It just seemed like the thing to do. There were several houses lining the shore, and we were undoubtedly seen by their inhabitants. Which made it even better.

But naked swimming is not as fringe as some puritanical readers out there might like to think. John Quincy Adams, the sixth president of the United States, was a devoted skinny dipper. Whenever he had the chance, he'd go out before dawn and do it in the Potomac. Many years later, in the 1960s, it was standing policy at the YMCA for swimming to be done in the nude, before women were allowed in.

There was nothing sexual or rebellious about it. Like my skinny dipping, it just seemed like a reasonable thing to do. I mention this because, from the American viewpoint at least, it seems to be about as close to a cultural parallel as there is to the Japanese bathing mentality. In the Japanese bath, getting naked, in and of itself, generates no big rush. It's just what you do before you get in the water.

Well, except sometimes. There is, at times, that element of being on display. Despite their walls, many outdoor baths are clearly visible to the non-bathers nearby. Jigokudani, or Hell's Valley, is famous worldwide because its bubbling hot waters are home to a large band of Japanese macaques. The snow monkeys, as they are called, are just a short hike through the woods from a tiny village dotted with hot spring inns and a very basic ski resort whose big moment came in 1998, when it was used as the venue for the Winter Olympics half-pipe snowboarding competition. Tens of thousands of people make the trek to the monkey park each year.

A few years ago, I was one of them. I'd been to the reserve before. But, intrigued by a guidebook that suggested the possibility of actually getting in a hot spring with the monkeys, I went to the inn by the river on the edge of the park and was told to go down a flight of wooden stairs, undress in the changing room, and then proceed through a pair of sliding doors, beyond which would be a very hot outdoor bath. The monkeys, I was informed, would sometimes see someone bathing out there and join them out of curiosity, or maybe in the hope of snagging a meal. I was sternly warned not to take anything even resembling food with me. The monkeys can get pretty grabby.

I did as I was told. I went down the stairs, found the changing room, stripped naked, and went through the sliding doors out into a blinding sun and the white-out of a snow-covered hillside. With my bucket for scooping up water from the bath to wash myself off with and my towel in hand, I blinked a few times.

When my eyes adjusted, I realized there was no fence. No partition. I was facing the world, full frontal. Across the river was the main road, crawling with cars. Beyond that, the trail led out from the woods to the gate of the park, where a line of tourists stood waiting to pay their entrance fee.

They might as well have skipped the ticket. I was now their entertainment for the day.

From nature by W. Heine.

P. S. Duval & Co. Philad.

Desperate for cover, I jumped into the tiny bath. It was scalding. I reflexively jumped out again and probably shrieked as I clumsily ran for the sliding doors, then ran back to get my bucket. I was freezing and boiling and red all over. Somewhere off in the distance, I believe I heard a monkey cackle.

And, I admit, it was kind of a kick. Deep down inside, dreading exposure all the while, we love to strut our stuff.

My name is Eric. And I am an exhibitionist.

BUT ENOUGH ABOUT me. We are talking culture here.

Being an American, when I think of going naked, or about nudity in general, I naturally think of nudism. And despite Japan's long history of socially-acceptable clothlessness, I have found that nudism in the Western sense—with its organizations, philosophical undertones and emphasis on being a social statement—is a really, really alien concept to the Japanese.

Of course, it didn't start off all that well in the West, what with that whole Adam and Eve episode. But that was by no means the end of the story. According to Corey Mangold, president of the International Naturists' Association, a California-based nudist group that claims 14,000 members worldwide, the true foundations of what he calls "nude recreation and social nudism" started in Ancient Egypt under Pharaoh Akhen-Aton (1385–1353 B.C.).

"It was during these times that students in Greece exercised and received their education in the nude," he notes on the society's homepage. "Also, most athletes played in the nude, including the early Olympic Games in Greece." (It is a little known fact, outside of nudist circles, that the root of gymnasium—*gymnos*—means "nude.")

The Golden Age of naked gallivanting didn't last long. The rise of Christianity pretty much put the kibosh on nude recreation. Outdoors, anyway. But over the past century, it has come back, with Europe—much more than

America, where it tends to be concentrated in California and Florida—establishing itself as the nudist bastion.

The modern nudist movement has its origins in Germany, where it was seen as a counterbalance to the stresses of modern, industrial life. In 1903, the world's first nudist park opened near Hamburg. But when the Nazis took over, they pretty much shut German nudism down. Among other things, Hitler probably had body image issues.

Today France, Italy, Spain and others have nude beaches all up and down their coasts. On sunny days, Scandinavians bare themselves in city parks, and nudism is also big in the Netherlands.

JAPAN, MEANWHILE, has had a very separate trajectory. The country is hardly a haven for nudists. There are no nude beaches here, at least not with legal sanction, nor are there any nudist colonies or nudist movements with any kind of a following. And this in a country where even the National Tug-of-War Association can claim support in the tens of thousands.

As we've already noted, mixed bathing has a long tradition in Japan. It was mentioned in an ancient chronicle of history and folklore called the *Izumo Fudoki*, and thus has roots that reach back at least as far as the sixth century and probably much further. In the heat of summer, peasants worked in virtual nudity. Women went topless in the fields. Even toward the end of the feudal era, townspeople would walk to the public bath in the raw.

"It's very complicated," explained Shinobu Machida, the sento expert. "Because we are an island nation, there was a feeling that we were all one family and thus there was less resistance to a certain amount of nudity in certain situations," he said. "Shinto and our style of Buddhism are also very tolerant of exposing the body, much more so than the Buddhism on the Asian continent."

The clothing clash with the West was inevitable. In 1853, Commodore Perry led a squadron of four ships into Tokyo Bay and demanded the Emperor sign a "friendship treaty." He was rebuffed, but returned the next year with a seven-ship fleet and 1,600 men. It was an offer Japan could hardly refuse.

On March 31, 1954, a treaty promising a "permanent friendship" between the two countries was signed in the port of Kanagawa, not far from the capital. It was one of the last acts of the samurai rulers, and Japan's race to catch up with the West was about to begin in earnest. That included staying dressed in front of the ladies.

"When the men aboard Perry's ships arrived in Japan and saw mixed bathing, they were aghast," Machida said. "They called the Japanese 'barbarians.'" Other early Western visitors to Japan, particularly Christian missionaries, were also scandalized by the amount of skin they were seeing. The Meiji reformers, looking to transform their feudal society into a modern, civilized nation acceptable to the Western visitors, acted quickly to divide the sexes and put a lid on public nudity.

Nakedness in public, urinating on the streets, and mixed bathing were all banned in a law passed in 1872, less than a decade after the fall of the samurai. The law was basically ignored, however, forcing the imposition of a tougher ban in 1900.

While compliance to the earlier law involved only the flimsiest of partitions between the man's and women's sections of the bath, the latter law truly spelled the end of mixed bathing. It required walls. It was enforced. And it worked. A tradition was effectively killed.

Today there are no legal public bathhouses anywhere in the country that have a mixed naked bathing zone. The laws have never been applied very strictly to hot springs. Even so, many places like Yunessun, which are kind of a gray zone to begin with, employ swimsuits just to be safe.

"It's as though we have become more Western than the West," Machida said.

Urinating on the streets, meanwhile, is alive and well.

NOT ALL WESTERNERS found Japan's way of bathing offensive. João Rodrigues, a Portuguese Jesuit who lived in Japan from 1580 to 1610, was very impressed by the bathing practices of the wealthy. "The Japanese seem to excel everybody else in this matter, not only in the frequency with which they bathe during the day, but even more so in the cleanliness and dignity which they observe in that place," he wrote.

He added that although it was the custom for "pages" to be in attendance (a practice in public baths that lasted well into modern times), shy guests could bring their own so as not to be looked upon by strangers. He also noted that "when many guests go into the sudatorium or bathe together, they observe great courtesies and compliments." The fact that they were naked as jaybirds didn't seem to bother him.

Basil Hall Chamberlain, a Brit who served as a professor at the University of Tokyo in the late 1800s and is credited with being the first foreigner to write a book on Japanese grammar, was also a supporter of the Japanese bath scene, going so far as to say that "cleanliness is one of the few original items of Japanese civilization."

"Cleanliness is more esteemed by the Japanese than our artificial Western prudery," he wrote in his turn-of-the-century book, *Japanese Things; Being Notes on Various Subjects Connected With Japan.* "As the editor of the *Japan Mail* [a newspaper of the time] has well said, the nude is seen in Japan, but it is not looked at."

Chamberlain makes a good point. Though the spin-off industry of bath-related sex was already well-established by the time of the reformers, and had been an issue with the samurai government before them, it has always been something of an exception—a tidal pool in the sea of Japan's bathing culture.

Most of the time, communal bathing just wasn't a sexual endeavor. The truth is, unless presented in the right way, nudity—total, unprettified nakedness—is a big turnoff. More than many cultures, the Japanese have long understood that. Just look at their erotic art. Those courtesans and incredibly well-endowed warriors in the sexually explicit *shunga* woodblock prints were almost always doing it with their clothes on. It added an extra dimension. It spoke of rank, of passion, of haste maybe, of a story behind the act that makes the scene so much more provocative. Nudes weren't much of a presence in Japanese art until the late 1800s, and then, again, it was largely in imitation of the West.

In the context of a socially accepted, commonplace routine, the sexiness of mixed bathing can be easily drowned out, and I think it is conceivable that for most Japanese of yore, most of the time, the turn on of seeing the opposite sex naked remained safely submerged.

But from about the time that mixed bathing was banned—making it officially naughty—it became sexy. And it was at about that time that Japan truly joined the ranks of the civilized.

AS THE YEAR 2005 came to a close, the popular *Weekly Playboy* magazine (no relation to the Hugh Hefner empire) lamented what it claimed was the accelerating demise of the mixed bath. Experts quoted figures to back up the speed with which mixed baths were vanishing from the landscape, replaced most often by gender-specific facilities, or, even worse in the eyes of *Weekly Playboy*, by swimsuit areas.

Officials had virtually doomed the free mingling of the sexes, the magazine claimed, by establishing guidelines in 1991 that discouraged

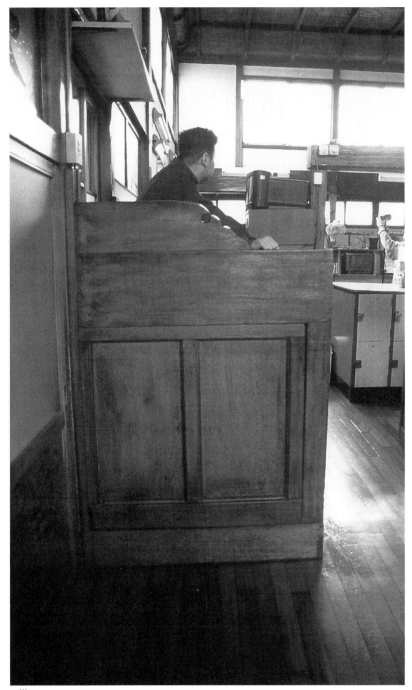

the construction of mixed areas in any new hot spring facility, meaning that most resorts opening after that year were compelled to split their baths down gender lines. But the law also hit the older hot springs: Owners seeking new licenses, or planning to hand down their inns to the next generation, had to play by the new rules. The water-tainting scandal that rocked the industry just after the turn of the millennium was the final blow. Officials started a general crackdown, pressuring resorts to play it by the book.

But there was a more important reason why mixed bathing was on its way out. Men. Libidinous men.

Tadanori Matsuda, founder of the Japan Hot Springs Research Institute and a professor of balneology at Sapporo International University, was quoted by *Weekly Playboy* as saying that there is an increasingly "lecherous attitude" among single male bathers, with some seeking out a vantage point facing the exit of the women's changing room and others sitting in the bath for hours on end, "carrying water bottles so they don't dehydrate."

"Mixed bathing, in which complete strangers could enjoy hot springs amid calmness and harmony, is a distinctive feature of Japan," he told the magazine. "It has a history of at least thirteen hundred years. It's outrageous that some mindless people are destroying this tradition."

But it's not especially surprising. A part of virtually no one's daily routine anymore, and the target of official disdain, mixed bathing has become the stuff of fantasy. With no nagging reality to drag the Japanese male's imagination back down to earth, they are free to imagine that mixed bathing actually means bathing amid beautiful, receptive young women who are really looking for sex. Where once there might have been scattered mental images of Grandma or the fat old ladies from the market, there is now a whole genre of pornography. Hot springs porn is, in fact, one of the more established niches in this country. It has gotten to the point where Web searches of "Japan Hot Springs" can often digress rapidly into a list of adult sites far removed from the realm of tourism or balneology. *Weekly Playboy* itself isn't averse to carrying photos of women at hot springs that suggest a whole lot more heat than mere water can convey.

Blame it on four billion years of evolution. Just as people in general are hard-wired to find faces in nearly any pattern imaginable, men are designed to find the promise of sex in just about everything they see. And by making it dirty and hard to come by, the official bans on nudity could only have had one outcome as far as the male psyche was concerned.

But as anyone who has been to a mixed bath knows, they are usually either empty, or populated exclusively by men. Usually wrinkly old men. If women are there at all, they are usually old too. Though the number and population of the mixed zones is dwindling, the better resorts and inns now tend to have private baths that either come with the room or can be rented out by the hour.

AS I SAT AMONGST my menagerie of naked men, I was thinking that maybe the incursion of swimsuits into the bath is a good thing.

Purists, of course, hate it. The arguments against swimwear are made regularly in the pages of the hot springs literature, where it is treated, a priori, as a crime against nature and humankind, or more accurately, *mankind*, and in the popular men's magazines, where the topic is mainly just an excuse to run some racy photos.

But, having been on both sides in the baths at Yunessun, I could definitely see the argument for modesty. There was something dour about the men's area. It was oddly unnatural. When there are few people in the bath, it doesn't much matter whether they are all men or women. The natural setting and the shared purpose of immersion tend to overwhelm all extraneous thoughts and concerns.

But when it gets too crowded, the artificiality of a one-gender bath becomes unavoidable, and very disconcerting. All the unilateral nakedness, when it gets too in-your-face, stops being part of the hoped-for return to nature and instead becomes a mockery of it. It becomes embarrassing.

A common feature at baths in Japan is a small hand towel, which is generally used to cover oneself when walking to and from the waters, and then placed on the top of the head when inside. Normally, it's a detail that goes unnoticed. I often go without them. At Yunessun, however, even the strategically placed towels—which were distributed to all—failed to create the illusion of comfortable nakedness.

Everything was just way too out there. Too exposed. Too, well, abundant. The contrast was impossible to miss. The swimsuit zone, though less tasteful in design, was much more upbeat. There was a normal mix of people. There were children, women of all ages, fathers, grandfathers. There was a sense of fun in the air. Oddly enough, it was this non-liberated, clothed side that had a feeling of abandon. And its sexlessness, though just as contrived, was much more comfortable than the men's side.

This struck me as especially interesting. Being a heterosexual male, I am predestined to be attracted to women. There is no switch to turn that off. But during the hours that I spent in mixed baths there, I didn't see a woman whom I found to be sexy. Not one.

I'm sure there were some around. That wasn't it. It was the environment. The situation. There was just something in the way it all worked that suppressed my normal male urge to be aroused by the female flesh that surrounded me.

Would it have worked without the swimsuits? Hard to say. But perhaps that's what it was like to be in the baths of old.

外国人の方の入場をお断りいたします

JAPANESE ONLY

ПРОСИМ ИНОСТРАННЫХ ГРАЖДАН НЕ
ВХОДИТЬ В ПОМЕЩЕНИЕ

VII

THE BATTLE OF
THE NORTH

*How drunken sailors, angry locals and an American-born activist
turned a sleepy Hokkaido town
into a symbol of civil rights denied.
Is the bath the last bastion of naked racism?*

AS A JOURNALIST based in Tokyo for more than twenty years,
I have traveled this country far and wide. I have flown to the tiny isle of
Yonaguni, so close to Taiwan that the radio stations all seem to be in Chinese. I've sailed to five of the seven islands of Izu. I've been to the temples
of Kyoto more times than I can remember. I've interviewed gangsters in
Osaka, watched three different volcanoes erupt, strolled the pebbled paths
of the Grand Shrines of Ise, watched the island of Okinawa fade away from
the backseat of a U.S. F-15 fighter.

Anywhere there has been news in this country, I've gone. But I've never
been to the snowy city of Otaru. And I've never been turned away from a
public bath. And I missed a huge story that involved both.

I'm not sure exactly how that happened. Everybody else covered it. The
story had everything a journalist could want. It pitted a group of foreigners
against indignant local townspeople. It got ugly. It got personal. It involved

allegations of drunken sailors swaggering around naked, swinging bottles of booze and swimming hand-in-hand. There was courtroom drama. Other than maybe a pregnant nun or a UFO landing, what more could you ask for?

It wasn't just tabloid fodder, though. The battle went all the way to the Supreme Court, and raised questions about how seriously Japan respects its written commitments to international law and fundamental human rights.

But most of all, it involved a bath.

THE SNOW IN OTARU—a city of 144,000 on the island of Hokkaido that is perhaps best known for its fish market or maybe its claim to have the world's largest steam-powered clock—starts to fall in November, and often keeps falling until March. By spring, it can get as deep as ten feet.

Prior to 1999, that was just about all anybody who didn't live there cared to know about Otaru. Like the rest of Hokkaido, it was cold and snowy and so far north that its port was full of Russians. It was, in fact, full of lots of crazy, drunken Russian sailors.

Japan's relations with Russia have always been tricky. On February 8, 1904, the two countries went to war over their conflicting ambitions in Korea and Manchuria. Reacting to the way that Moscow was muscling in on its own claims to the Liaotung Peninsula, Japan, fresh off a victory in the Sino-Japan War, launched a surprise torpedo attack on the Russian naval squadron at Port Arthur, in southern Manchuria. The Japanese army then overran Korea, cut off the Russians who remained in Port Arthur, and drove northward. As the Russians got supplies from the Trans-Siberian Railroad, their position improved and the war began to look like a stalemate. The battle for Mukden alone left the Russians with 90,000 casualties, and another 71,000 for Japan.

But after less than two years, Japan emerged victorious. A treaty brokered in Portsmouth, New Hampshire, by President Theodore Roosevelt in September 1905, forced Russia to give up its expansionist efforts in East Asia and, among other things, cede the southern half of Sakhalin Island, which is just north of Hokkaido. It was a huge humiliation for Russia, marking the first defeat in modern times of a Western power by an Asian nation. Japan, now a major player, was emboldened in its eventually disastrous dash toward military adventurism.

Today, relations are still colored by territory disputes. In the closing days of World War II, the Soviet Red Army occupied several small islands between Hokkaido and Sakhalin. Japan has refused to back down on its claim to the islands, which it calls the Northern Territories, and the two countries have never signed a peace treaty formally ending their World War II hostilities.

Even so, the fall of the Soviet Union and the end of the Cold War brought a rapid expansion in trade between them, especially on Hokkaido, which was closest to the new economic frontline. Ports like Otaru were suddenly swollen with Russian sailors and traders, who came to sell fish and buy used cars, which they could make a tidy profit on back home. By the early 1990s, some thirty thousand Russian sailors were flowing through Otaru each year.

That there would be some friction was probably inevitable. Before long, incidents were being reported in taxis, restaurants, bars. And, since we are talking about Japan after all, baths.

In the frigid climate of Otaru, baths are an inviting escape. But when problems started cropping up here, they got nasty in more ways than one. To the chagrin of the townspeople, the Russian visitors developed a reputation for not washing themselves off properly before getting in, or washing themselves after they got in, which is even worse. Some carried vodka bottles in with them. Others bathed in their underpants, which is totally unforgivable if you are Japanese. By the summer of 1993, the situation had reached its boiling point.

A new Russia-Japan war was declared, in front of the hot spring bath of Osupa. It was simple and in English.

"Japanese Only," it said.

Other baths soon joined in. When the hot spring Yu-no-Hana opened in July 1998, it did so with an open policy of refusing all foreigners, claiming that the ill-behaved Russians had driven another establishment, the Green Sauna, out of business because local townspeople were afraid to go there.

To publicize its policy, Yu-no-Hana, a large, family-oriented hot spring, also prominently displayed a "Japanese Only" sign outside its doors. But theirs was more sophisticated than Osupa's. It was written in English, Japanese and Russian.

The battle had begun. But, this time, it wasn't the Russians who would take up arms.

ON SEPTEMBER 19, 1999, David Aldwinckle went to Yu-no-Hana with his wife, children, and several friends. His Japanese wife and a Chinese friend went in first to buy tickets, while Aldwinckle "gawked at the sign outside."

"I had never seen such a brazen example of xenophobia on such an earnest-looking establishment," he wrote in a blow-by-blow description of the confrontation on his Web site, which has become something of a first point of reference for foreigners facing legal or social problems in Japan.

Aldwinckle, of course, knew the sign would be there. Familiar with, and infuriated by, the bath's Japanese only policy, he and his friends were deliberately testing the waters. He had laid out a game plan. Aldwinckle had carefully balanced his group with Caucasians, Asians, his Japanese wife, and his half-Japanese children. And he had a strategy. All participants that day were told not to give out "a traceable name," and to let ringleader Aldwinckle have the final word.

They even had a rule book.

"DON'T GET ANGRY (may be interpreted against us later as being 'threatening') OR SMILE (may show that we're here for a lark, having fun harassing private companies)," the instructions to the group began. "DO KEEP A STRAIGHT POKER FACE (*sumashita kao*) and if you show any emotion, make it sadness and disappointment. Appealing to pity works better here, in my experience. . . .

"DON'T EVER TOUCH ANYBODY. As in America, lay a finger on anybody and it's assault. If they block your entry, do not push. Do not plan to enter by any means. DO JUST STAND THERE AND TALK ONE-BY-ONE (take turns because it is less threatening than a flurry of comments all at once). We are not here to cause trouble."

The encounter played out pretty much as expected. Aldwinckle's Japanese wife, Fumiko, and the Chinese woman were able to buy the tickets. But when Aldwinckle and the others in the group tried to follow, a young man working at the counter informed them that they were not allowed to go any further.

Help was called in. According to Aldwinckle's account of the meeting, the manager, a haggard-looking middle-age Japanese man, offered the following explanation, as about thirty people looked on:

"Foreigners, especially Russian sailors, have bad manners. They come in here and jump into the baths and splash water everywhere," he said. "They don't wash the soap off before they get into the hot water and sometimes even get in with their underpants on. They swim hand-in-hand and talk in loud voices. Sometimes they're drunk or carrying vodka bottles, and because their bodies are big and they don't understand Japanese it can be hard to reason with them or get them to leave. They are frightening to our customers, who often complain to the management that if there are Russians here they won't come back."

The manager then claimed that the ban had been put in place in the interest of being fair. "We can't just ban Russians in particular, so we ban all foreigners out of fairness," he told Aldwinckle and the others. "We have a business to run, and we can't let people in who will spoil the atmosphere of our onsen."

Long story short, Aldwinckle ended up taking his bath elsewhere that day. Then he and two others who were refused entry at Yu-no-Hana went back home and filed a lawsuit.

FROM THE START, THE media was involved in the showdown. A Japanese reporter was with Aldwinckle when he made his visit. The local newspaper, with little else in the way of significant local news, covered the story aggressively. But this story really had legs, and soon went far beyond the scope of local news.

It went national. Then international. On Aldwinckle's Web-site, he has posted numerous clips from all of the major Japanese media, not to mention the *New York Times*, The Associated Press, the *Los Angeles Times*, the *South China Morning Post*, the BBC . . . you name it.

It became a diplomatic issue as well. The German Embassy piped in with a complaint; one of the plaintiffs, Olaf Karthaus, was German. (The third, Ken Sutherland, was American.) In a letter to the mayor of Otaru, the embassy wrote, "considering the traditional and friendly relations between Germany and Japan, we see this discrimination towards a German citizen based only upon appearance or nationality as a very serious problem."

In 2002, the bathhouse battle even made its way into the U.S. State Department's annual report on human rights practices, which said that, as a result of widespread media attention, appeals by the Justice Ministry, and an antidiscrimination campaign waged by nongovernmental organizations, "several businesses in Hokkaido lifted their bans against foreigners."

It went on to report: "In February in Hokkaido police investigated death threats made against a foreign-born naturalized citizen who had sued both a bathhouse for refusing him entrance on the basis of race and the Otaru Municipal Government for failing to take measures to stop discriminatory entrance policies."

Otaru had hit the big time.

WITH THE ACCUSATIONS of naked racism now out in the open, emotions got as hot as Yu-no Hana's waters. Supporters of the onsen and other establishments with similar policies argued that it was reasonable from a business perspective to ban foreigners if a foreign clientele was scaring away other customers. In the Japanese media there was, initially at least, a lot of sympathy for Yu-no-Hana's position. It was a kind of wink-wink, nod-nod, those-foreigners-can-be-a-real-handful attitude that a lot of people could relate to.

There was also more than a touch of indignation over the manner in which Aldwinckle had created this battle, and his very tenacious pursuit of Yu-no-Hana.

In a letter to the editor of the *Hokkaido Shimbun*, the local daily that had covered the story from the very start, a thirty-three-year-old housewife said that although she felt sorry that all foreigners had to pay for the bad behavior of a small group of Russians, she also felt the bathhouse owners had to do something.

"This all came about because of the ill manners of some Russians in the bath," she wrote. "The public bathhouse operators are the victims here, and it is odd that they are being treated like the bad guys."

Even some long-term foreign residents took this view. Back when the brouhaha had just started bubbling, Gregory Clark, an Australian president of a Japanese university and well-known social commentator in Japan, offered these opinions in an editorial published by the *Japan Times*, a conservative English-language newspaper, on Christmas day, 1999:

"There is something very one-sided about the way so many outsiders want to see Japan as a den of racist iniquity," he wrote. "Almost every foreigner here must at some time or other have felt the extraordinary courtesy and honesty the Japanese can show to outsiders. Is that supposed to be part of some racist plot?

"The critics are now focusing on an Otaru bathhouse keeper who sought to keep out visiting Russian seamen. Many of these people are delightful. Even so, the fact remains that people who have just arrived from Sakhalin on unsanitary, rust-bucket boats are bound to cause problems (*meiwaku*) in Japanese bathhouses. In Japan's person-oriented value system, causing meiwaku is a major sin."

Clark granted that there are times when anti-foreign sentiment in Japan can turn ugly, but said that was "usually just the flip side of the instinctive sensitivities that lead so many other Japanese to be unduly pro-*gaijin* [foreigner]." "Even at its militaristic worst, the Japanese approach to foreigners was ambiguous," he wrote. "Japanese nationalists would vent cruel hatred on other Asians seen as unfriendly. But they would then turn round and embrace those whom they thought were pro-Japan.

"To demand that Japanese observe our value system, while pouring scorn on theirs, is the worst kind of racism," he concluded.

Well, okay. I suppose that's one way of looking at it. Not wanting to sound arrogant or overbearing, I will reserve judgment. Though I bet it kind of sucked to be on the receiving end of that cruel hatred.

Aldwinckle, of course, stressed that he wasn't responsible for the actions of the ill-behaved Russians. He had caused no trouble. He knew how to conduct himself in the bath. He was merely seeking access to a bath that was open to everybody else.

"I think it started off relatively simply," he told me. "You had a perceived problem—ill-mannered Russian sailors—and you took a simple measure against it: banning them, er, well, everyone who looks like them, er, well, everyone who is not like us . . .

"The problem was that all the intellectual sleight of hand that one had to conjure up to keep the system justifiable whenever people began asking questions was ultimately not tenable. And the more people realized it, the more desperate people became to find more contrived reasons: Japan's bathing culture is unique, foreigners can't understand us and we can't understand them, foreigners and Japanese are discernible on sight.

"Yet for many the logic still washed, pardon the pun," he said.

Aldwinckle, a California native and Cornell graduate who is a university instructor and owns a house on Hokkaido, became a naturalized Japanese citizen on October 10, 2000. His name is now Arudou Debito, and he was the naturalized Japanese the State Department had referred to in its rights report.

That was a story in itself. A couple of weeks after becoming a Japanese citizen, Arudou née Aldwinckle promptly went to Yu-no-hana with his papers. But he was still turned away because, he was told; "We at the counter know you are a Japanese, but our customers won't . . . so we have to refuse you admission."

♨

EVENTUALLY, THE COURTS sided with Aldwinckle, Karthaus, and Sutherland. Well, in spirit, anyway.

In 2002, the Sapporo High Court ruled that Yu-no-Hana had discriminated against the three and ordered the bath to pay each of them one million yen in compensation. The ruling held that the bathhouse was guilty of "discriminating too much," not explicitly for discriminating against them based on their race.

In April 2005, the Supreme Court ruled that the city of Otaru, who the three were also suing, could not be held responsible for the discriminatory policy of the baths there. In an editorial on the Sapporo High Court verdict, the *Japan Times* came out with a position very different from that expressed by Clark in its pages just a few years earlier.

"Many Japanese seem to have a fixed idea of what a Japanese should look like," it said. "They have no trouble digesting the reality of a Japanese-Peruvian or Japanese-American, but reverse the words and they have a strong resistance to the notion of Peruvian-Japanese or American-Japanese." It went on to say that, with upward of thirty thousand international marriages in Japan each year, such thinking will need to change: "It is time for the Japanese to recognize that the age of diversity has hit home." The editorial was also highly critical of the official government position on discrimination.

Rights activists in Japan have long stressed that one of the biggest obstacles they face is the lack of a law that specifically bans racism or racial discrimination. Because there was no domestic law to protect him, Aldwinckle had to sue under the somewhat convoluted claim that rights guaranteed under a United Nations convention that Japan signed were being violated.

The *Times* noted this as well. "Following the spread of neo-Naziism in Europe, the [International Convention on the Elimination of All Forms of Racial Discrimination] was adopted by the U.N. General Assembly in 1965.

Japan eventually ratified the convention thirty years later in 1995—the 146th country, and the last of the advanced countries, to do so.

"Even then, Japan was slow to establish related domestic legislation. In March 2001, in a final opinion paper on Japan, the U.N. Committee on the Elimination of Racial Discrimination strongly urged Japan to enact legislation on the elimination of racial discrimination that carries penalties."

But times change slowly. The *Times* editorial then raised an issue that is almost always somehow tacked onto any discussion of foreigners in Japan— the specter of rising crime. It quoted a report that had recently been issued by the police saying that as the number of foreigners entering Japan had increased over the past decade, the number of crimes involving foreigners had risen 2.3 times and the number of arrests had jumped 1.6 times.

Oddly, it wrapped up with this: "Such problems will not be solved by harboring a dislike of new neighbors and shutting them out. We must build a society that gently and kindly embraces different peoples and minorities. It is important for each of us to be prepared. That should be the lesson of the Sapporo District Court case."

AS A LONG-TERM RESIDENT, and bather, myself, I suppose I'm a player in this little drama. And I have some personal opinions.

First off, it's an anomaly. Like I said at the outset, I've never been turned away from a bath. Except when I've dropped in for the first time at a small bathhouse where regulars are the rule, I've never even really felt that my presence was given much of a second thought. The response on the part of the Otaru bathhouse owners is the exception, not the rule. Circumstance, the local issues specific to that town at that time, clearly played a major role in their decision.

And those circumstances can be pretty vexing. I have seen more than my share of bad manners in the bath. And the offenders are indeed often foreigners, though there are sure as hell enough brutish Japanese to go around.

So, fact is, I'm with the timid townspeople of Otaru. I wouldn't want to bathe with a bunch of drunken and rowdy Russian sailors, either. Or, to be more exact, I wouldn't want to bathe with a bunch of drunken and rowdy creeps, whatever their nationality. You are pretty defenseless in a bath. It's the last place you want to feel threatened or intimidated.

But racism is racism. Aldwinckle—agitator or not—had every right to go into that bath. He wasn't drunk. He didn't look like a troublemaker. He spoke Japanese. He was reasonable and intelligent. He was with his family. When he went there after changing his citizenship, he even passed the "Japanese Only" standard.

The bathhouse management knew all that, and turned him—and his children—away just the same.

But does this whole bath imbroglio mean that Japan is racist? It is kind of a silly question, really. There are an awful lot of people that comprise Japan (Aldwinckle and perhaps even myself would need to be included) and they harbor an awfully wide variance of opinions. Plus, it is all relative. I mean, compared to what? The Deep South in the 1920s? Paris as seen from the eyes of an immigrant from the Middle East? The conditions faced by Aborigines in Australia?

I've been subject to some pretty blatant racism here. But it has mostly been in the form of ignorant, aggravating attitudes. For instance, I'll go into a fast-food joint and the person taking my order will insist on speaking to me in English, despite the fact that they can't really speak English. And that I have just made my order in perfectly understandable Japanese.

I can be the only non-Japanese on a subway train packed with thousands of people—or in a bath surrounded by Japanese—and feel totally at home. But what you realize, jarringly, at the fast-food counter is that some people aren't seeing you as just another person. They are seeing a white guy. A foreigner. And to them, you will never be anything more.

At the heart of it, that's pretty much what racism is all about, anywhere. In college, when I was still trying to figure out where I belonged in this society, my favorite book was Ralph Ellison's *Invisible Man*. To show my emphatic agreement, one lonely night in my dorm room I underlined the parts in the prologue when the protagonist talks about how people are bumping into him all the time because they won't acknowledge him, and how that makes him begin to want to start bumping them back.

"I am invisible, understand, simply because people refuse to see me. Like the bodiless heads you sometimes see in circus sideshows, it is as though I have been surrounded by mirrors of hard, distorting glass," he explains. "You wonder whether you aren't simply a phantom in other people's minds. Say, a figure in a nightmare that the sleeper tries with all his might to destroy."

What a perfect description. I still have that book.

But nobody's burning crosses in my yard.

Others in Japan face equally blatant—but far more than annoying—instances of racism. It can and does get very nasty when it is directed at the Koreans and Chinese who live here. Or at people from South Asia or the Middle East, whose numbers have risen dramatically over the past decade.

Since I can usually talk my way through the nonmalignant forms of racism that I face, maybe I'm too sanguine. The Otaru story at first turned me off. I didn't care much for the forced fight element. The Japanese, like everyone else, I imagine, really hate being set up like that, and I could see a backlash. And in a real narrow sort of way, it just wasn't a problem that I was facing in my own life. One of the first hot springs I ever went to was in Hokkaido, and I had a good time there, with a mixed bag of foreigners and Japanese. There was no friction. We all got along fine. Overall, I was doing okay on the bathing front. So why draw the guns?

But I have since come to appreciate the efforts of activists like Aldwinckle. And I also appreciate that the Japanese are often patient, welcoming hosts. Japan, in my opinion, is a great place to live.

And bathe.

YOU DON'T HEAR MUCH about the Russians in Otaru anymore. They are still up there and I guess they are still doing the things that sailors are wont to do when they are set loose on a foreign land where there is no dearth of booze and baths. But I think that the storm has passed. The "Japanese Only" signs have come down, and not just because of court orders. The media, as they are wont to do, have moved on.

Out of curiosity, I asked Aldwinckle, a heavyset, thick-featured man in his early forties, why he bothered. "I think this will be my epitaph," he said. "Somebody's got to do it. It might as well be me."

He acknowledged that, as some of his critics still complain, he had to go out of his way to seek out the Otaru bath, and that he has rarely been denied service anywhere in Japan. But, he noted, that isn't really the point.

"I have had only a few problems getting service in Japan," he said. "And yes, my investigating places which *do* have problems makes me more likely to encounter them than average. But there are problems with differential treatment based upon nationality out there, and whenever one encounters them, lots of people want to resolve them in a way that's satisfactory all around."

Talking it out, he said, works a little more than half the time. "Anyway, it's not a matter of number or degree," he added. "One case of racial discrimination is too many. It's just a matter of making sure that *that* is the root cause of the problem—not some other, talk-throughable misunderstanding—or else our legitimacy as a conscientious group is kaput."

That the case centered on a bath did add special sensitivities. "There are issues of sanitation, modesty, style, and culture all intertwined here," he said. But he stressed that discrimination by race in Japan is by no means limited to hot springs. Aldwinckle keeps a "rogues gallery" collection of photos of Japanese Only signs. He has them from stores, restaurants, bars, hotels, pachinko parlors, discos, even a boutique and a barber. They are found all over the country. The bathhouses of Otaru just happen to have been caught holding the ball.

But the Battle of the Bath isn't completely over. At the time of this writing, Aldwinckle was readying a new lawsuit, this time taking on the national government for allegedly not living up to its obligations under the U.N. convention to establish domestic laws to ensure that racism is not allowed in this country.

"Issues of racism or xenophobia are never simple," he wrote me from his Hokkaido home.

ODDLY ENOUGH, THERE is one group of Japanese for whom getting a good public soak is even more difficult than for drunken Russian sailors. And they are not making a fuss.

When I was just getting started in journalism, one of the beats I chose to pursue was organized crime—the notorious yakuza. It was a great beat. Japan has a very colorful underworld, and it was especially so back in the 1980s. These guys had no shame. They would swagger around, wear pins with the logos of their gangs right there on their lapels for anyone to see, congregate in headquarters with big signs out front saying exactly which gang they were with. They were often happy to do interviews, which made it very easy to cover them, though they got pretty self-serving and rarely talked about the nuts and bolts of business. One of my sources, a mid-level boss with the Yamaguchi-gumi, Japan's biggest gang, used to send me New Year's cards with the syndicate's logo embossed in gold in one corner.

All that has changed quite a bit. After a couple of police officers were killed by gangsters in southern Japan, the laws were revised in 1992 to make it harder for the mob to operate quite as openly as they had been. The underworld was sent back underground, where their activities are less subject to public scrutiny.

Before all that happened, though, I was having dinner with my Yamaguchi-gumi source one night and I noticed that he had a tattoo that stopped at his wrists. It was, he told me, a full-body tattoo, and most old-school gangsters had them.

I knew that quite a few hot springs, saunas, bathhouses, and shower rooms at country clubs and sports centers post signs banning anyone with a tattoo from using their facilities—with the express purpose of keeping these guys from frightening their customers away.

He was a fairly in-your-face kind of guy. He wasn't shy. And he loved walking into a room and seeing the way people reacted to his shiny lapel pin. So I asked him if he had ever tried to go to a public bath.

This is what he said:

"They don't want me, so I've never gone. Why bother?"

He then ordered a plate full of little sausages and gave me a detailed description of how and why he had to chop off the tip of his little finger, another old-school gangster tradition.

But I will save that story for another book.

xxv

VIII

AFTERGLOW

*A visit to a small village
where the measure of a good bath is done in becquerels.
How radon has gone from miracle cure
to carcinogen and, perhaps, back to miracle cure*

SUMMER IN JAPAN is just plain oppressive. After the month-long rainy season ends sometime in July, a swelter sets in. The benign, let's-hit-the-beach implications of the word "sunshine" don't do justice to what then fills the skies.

"Radiation" is a much better word. The summer sun's menacing ultraviolet rays, nasty and mean-spirited, pound down, seeking out the unprotected, the fair-skinned, the bald. The air, meanwhile, is so thick with humidity that sweat begins not just to trickle but to pour after even a few steps outdoors. For dramatic effect, it seems, typhoons lash the archipelago with increasing frequency as the season wears on. With their howling winds and buckets of rain, the storms are normally more of a nuisance than a danger, and they are over in a day or so. But they have one universally recognized benefit—they provide a welcome, albeit brief, respite from the scorching summer sun.

The real weight of the Japanese summer, however, is the weight of the nation's past. August is the month of death, devastation, and defeat.

Mid-month, millions of people vacate the cities and head back to their hometowns to mark the ancient Festival of the Dead, or *O-Bon*, when, according to Buddhist thought, the spirits of the ancestors make a brief return to check up on the world of the living. The timing of the festival is a little eerie.

It was noon on August 15, 1945, when the late Emperor Hirohito made an unprecedented announcement over the radio declaring that Japan had lost the war, or, as he chose to put it, must accept the unacceptable. Because Japan hasn't fought a war since, the significance of the surrender remains powerful, and its anniversary is an emotional summer event. Adding to its impact, the defeat is observed smack in the middle of O-Bon—a fitting coincidence considering the tens of millions of Japanese who died in the fighting, and the tens of millions more who died fighting them, before Hirohito's fateful address.

But two even more poignant anniversaries come first. On August 6, tens of thousands of people gather in Hiroshima to remember the world's first atomic bomb attack. Three days later, crowds gather to commemorate the obliteration of Nagasaki the second atomic target. The two bombings killed well over two hundred thousand people and, undoubtedly, hastened the collapse of Japan's war machine.

In Hiroshima one hot, sunny afternoon to cover a recent anniversary, I found myself talking to Charles Waldren, Ph.D., a tall, gray-haired man with bright blue eyes and a scientist's slow, articulate manner of speech. Waldren is one of the foremost experts on what radiation does to living organisms. For decades before coming to Hiroshima, he studied its effects on people, dogs, horses, and cats.

"That's right, cats get cancer too," he said. "It's sad to see."

As chief of research at Hiroshima's Radiation Effects Research Foundation, a large but somewhat drab, bunker-like series of laboratories atop a tree-covered hill overlooking the city, Waldren was in charge of a unique project.

Two years after the bombing of Hiroshima, U.S. researchers—backed by the Atomic Energy Agency and the Occupation-run Japanese government—put together data on one hundred thousand A-bomb survivors; they were the cohort for a study designed to track their health for the rest of their lives, in order to determine just how much the radiation they absorbed would increase their long-term risk of disease in general, and, of course, cancer in particular. Sixty years after the bombing, the study was still going strong, with forty thousand of the cohort, now with an average age of seventy-one, still alive.

Waldren, seventy-one himself, described the results as counterintuitive. Although there was a clear link between very high exposure and cancer, Hiroshima A-bomb survivors over the years have proven to be only 5 percent more likely to develop cancers than your average New Yorker, he said—adding that smokers are at far greater risk of succumbing to cancer than people who were relatively close to the hypocenter at the time of the blast.

"Of course, for individuals who develop cancer this is small consolation," he said. "But I think the data is very encouraging."

Since I had him talking, I asked what he thought of Japan's many radioactive hot springs. I was going to one the next day and wanted to know if he thought there was anything to all the claims that the radiation in the baths was potentially healthy.

He smiled.

"It's like taking a hammer to a thousand-dollar watch, hoping to fix it," he said. "They're not good for you."

ACCORDING TO ITS brochures, the secluded village of Misasa, in the secluded prefecture of Tottori on the Japan Sea, bursts to life with two exciting and unique festivals each year. The "Flower Water" festival, loosely associated with the arrival of spring, is in early May and climaxes with, for reasons unexplained, a tug-of-war. The second festival is held on August third and fourth, just days before Hiroshima remembers the A-bomb.

It's called the *Kyurii-sai*. And, though not terribly exciting, it is unique.

Misasa is perhaps the only city outside of Poland, or possibly France, that holds an annual celebration in honor of Maria Sklodowska-Curie, better known as Madam Marie Curie, who, with her husband, Pierre Curie, and Henri Becquerel, won the 1903 Nobel Prize in physics for the discovery of polonium and radium. She later received the Nobel chemistry prize, in 1911. Only one other person has won two Nobels in different fields—Linus Pauling (chemistry and peace).

A pioneer in the field of radioactivity, Curie was notoriously devoted to her research, and her devotion probably killed her—she died in 1934 of leukemia. Even her notes were so steeped in radioactivity that they had to be decontaminated before being released to the public by her granddaughter.

Still, in this picturesque little village so far removed from Curie's homeland, radium and radon, a gas that emanates from radium as it decays, are as good as gold. For centuries, the plentiful, radon-heavy waters that bubble up to constantly replenish the countless natural wells here have truly been the village's lifeblood.

With the possible exception of a spa or two in Eastern Europe, Misasa is quite likely the world's foremost radon hot springs resort. It is certainly the most lucrative.

Hideaki Ohashi, a young, sharply dressed man whose family has run Ryokan Ohashi, a popular inn, for four generations, is pretty typical of the

Misasa villagers in that he is singularly unimpressed by the festival—which everyone in town, even the organizers, seems to write off as a halfhearted promotional gimmick.

I was told by several villagers that there is, in fact, a statue of Curie somewhere in Misasa, and that French diplomats have been known to place flowers before it. But, for all intents and purposes, the festival has nothing to do with Madam Curie. Instead, its main event is a contest to see who can with their bare hands catch the most fish in the shallow, rocky Mitoku River, which runs through the center of the village. Then there are some fireworks. And that's pretty much it.

When I visited, Ohashi was having nothing to do with the whole affair. "I don't know much about Madam Curie, other than that she discovered the stuff that radon comes from," he said after sinking into a sofa in the swank, century-old inn's otherwise traditionally Japanese-style lobby. "It's not that big a festival, anyway. It's not the kind of event that would draw many people from outside the area. It's more just for us. The one in May is much more fun."

Nevertheless, like most of the eight thousand villagers in Misasa, Ohashi's life revolves around the gas that Curie helped discover. The guests at his inn—and there are plenty—are there for the radon.

And Ohashi gladly gives the people what they want. In two indoor pools, set in a craggy grotto-style bath room, they soak in waters with three or more times higher radon levels than found normally in nature. Unlike many baths in Japan, these are the real deal. The spring water bubbles up slowly, naturally, from directly below the bathing pools. It's not pumped up or piped in from afar. And it's not recycled.

There is no particular smell. The waters are clear, and hot (145°F at the source), but not excessively so. Somewhat to my disappointment, there was no freakish blue-green glow. No mysterious aurora, no Geiger counters clicking away in a corner somewhere. Were it not for signs on the walls denoting the radioactive content of the baths, it would be impossible to guess that there was anything particularly out of the ordinary here at all.

The variety of ways to get exposed, however, was impressive. After a dip indoors, I went outside and soaked in another radioactive bath, this one heavy with thoron, a highly unstable gas produced by a different but related radioactive element, thorium. The setting is peaceful, with a view of the meandering Mitoku and Misasa's deep, verdant hills over a low bamboo fence. But lest anyone forget, a sign near the bath notes that researchers from Tokyo University years ago studied its thoron content and declared it was probably the highest in the world. "We're especially proud of that," Ohashi said.

Up a few steps from the outdoor bath is a sauna, which I discovered was full of steam made from radon-laden water. Perfect, another sign said, for inhaling.

Finally, to top it all off, I took a short walk and joined other radon-craving visitors who were getting an even more direct fix by simply drinking the stuff, straight out of the ground. Public baths around the village offer radon water gushing from spigots, free for the taking.

The public baths are only a few dollars a dip, but the private spas are notoriously pricey. Overnights, which include a multi-course dinner, start at around ¥20,000 and can easily climb to twice that—explaining why it is rare for visitors to stay long enough for the baths to have much of a physical impact. In the short-term, at least.

Even so, determined to experience Misasa to the fullest, I did it all. Radon. Thoron. Immersing, inhaling, imbibing. I even had a second cup. And a third. I was on a radon binge.

But nothing.

Of course, like most visitors, I was just there for a couple of days. But Ohashi, a healthy looking man in his mid-thirties, is a Misasa lifer. Not surprisingly, he swears by his baths.

"I've taken these baths every day since I was a kid," he said. "I feel great. I haven't caught a cold or had a fever for six years. That's what the baths do best. They bolster your immune system. It's called the hormesis effect. They also ease fatigue and muscle aches. There are other benefits, for women's problems, for example. And the skin. But the real benefit is to the immune system.

"People think of radiation and they think danger. But that's not true," he continued. "Low-level radiation, like what we are talking about here, is actually a good thing. People think radon gives you cancer. Here, it helps protect you from cancer. I had a guest who came here all the time who was cured of stomach cancer. And it was in a pretty advanced stage."

Such anecdotes are hard to substantiate. There are no doctors on duty here or at any of the other Misasa inns. No one measures or regulates how much is too much, nor tracks the progress of a bather actually seeking a cure to whatever it may be that ails him. In Misasa, the water's benefits are basically just accepted as a matter of faith. And that's the way it's been for about eight hundred years.

But not everyone is as sold on radon's wonders as the bathers of Misasa.

IN THE UNITED STATES, radon is seen as one of the devil's own minions. The gas is designated by the government as a highly dangerous carcinogen, and in 1988 the Indoor Radon Abatement Act authorized the Environmental Protection Agency to push for awareness of its risks and provide grants to efforts aimed at lowering radon levels in public places.

xxvi

A study by the National Academy of Sciences in the late 1990s estimated that between fifteen and twenty-two thousand Americans die annually of radon-related lung cancer, making it the second-leading cause of lung cancer after smoking.

The EPA recommends radon testing in all schools, and the Surgeon General has advocated testing for it in rooms below the third floor of all buildings. As one might expect, a lucrative business has sprung up in the detection and removal of radon from everything from corporate offices to basements in private homes.

But escaping the reach of radon isn't easy. According to an EPA public service fact sheet, the odorless, colorless, and tasteless gas is the primary source of exposure for humans to naturally occurring radiation. It's most familiar isotope, radon-222, is a decay product of uranium-238, which, surprisingly enough to most non-physicists, is actually found just about everywhere. When radon-222, which has a half-life of less than four days, releases alpha radiation it decays into polonium-218 (polonium was named after Curie's native Poland), then lead-214, bismuth-214, and so on until it finally hits the stable stopping point of lead-206.

Because it is a noble gas, meaning it doesn't combine with other chemicals, radon tends to move freely through the ground. It is most often found in places where the landscape is high in granite or phosphate, because that's where higher amounts of uranium and radium are to be expected. As the parent elements decay, the resulting radon gas spreads out, often dissolving in the nearest ground water. Radon quickly disperses when it comes in contact with air, so it is generally not found in high concentrations in lakes or rivers.

But it can reach high concentrations in subterranean pools, which, of course, is the case in Misasa. It also has a propensity to mass in shower or washing water in homes that use their own natural wells, as opposed to public reservoirs, where the water is much more likely to be treated, agitated, and exposed to open air.

So much for the physics. Here comes the sinister part. As radon decays, which is what radioactive materials do, the short-lived solid decay products—tiny bits of metal—can attach themselves to dust or other particles in the air. Though most of the radon we breathe in is simply exhaled right back out, it's these decay particles, which scientists affectionately call "daughters," that pose the problem. Instead of going back out into the air, radon's deadly daughters can get stuck on the lining of the lungs. While there, they continue to decay, releasing energy and potentially messing up the operation of the cells around them, thus damaging the surrounding lung tissue. Such damage can lead to cancer.

Drinking radon-heavy water also is risky, as it can expose the places it comes in contact with, such as the lining of the stomach, to similar damage scenarios. The risk is lower than with inhalation, though, because radon's daughters lose their energy more quickly in water.

Bottom line? "Radon has little practical use," the agency concludes. "There is no safe dose of radon—any exposure poses some risk of cancer."

IN THE EARLY 1900s, radioactive water was all the rage.

Setting the tone for three decades of popular radon fascination, eminent physicist J. J. Thompson, who discovered the electron, realized that radioactivity was common in well water, and in 1903 shared his observations in the journal *Nature*. Scientists and doctors soon began to see radioactivity as the active ingredient in all healing baths. It was, in the thinking of the times, like a spark that generated invigorating processes all through the body.

The radon boom, which hit its peak in the early 1930s, spawned a cottage industry of quack cures. Most were largely harmless and had far less of a radioactive punch than advertised. But others, unfortunately, had enough of a wallop to, literally, knock your jaw off.

One of the leading providers of fine radium products in the 1920s was Associated Radium Chemists, Inc., of New York, which sold an array of health care goods that included ARIUM radium tablets, various radium ointments and liniments, radium-laced dentrices, and even a radium hair tonic called "Kaparium."

But by no means did they have a corner on the market. Americans by that time were bathing in radium bath salts, brushing their teeth with radium toothpaste, resting their heads on radon pillows, wearing radium jockstraps, and seeking vigor in Radol, which actually had no radium or radon in it but did produce a nice blue glow inside its bottle. Until its inventor was jailed for fraud, that is.

Meanwhile, in the mushrooming radon haven of Bohemia, in what is now the Czech Republic, there was radium bread, baked with radon-laden water by the Hippmann-Blach bakery in St. Joachimstal, now Jachymov. In Germany, the health-conscious were adding radium bromide to their crackers, tea, and chocolate.

The *piece d'résistance*, however, had to be Vita Radium Suppositories. Produced by the Denver, Colorado-based Home Products Company, the suppositories were billed as a sort of radioactive Viagra. "Recommended for sexually weak men," the suppositories were, according to the labels on their boxes, supposed to be "restorers of sex and energizers for the nervous, glandular, and circulatory systems.

"These suppositories contain a result-producing amount of highly refined soluble radium carried in a cocoa butter base." Well, if it's in cocoa butter, why not?

Radon water also had a huge mass appeal, but because radon quickly dissipates into the air, making it impossible to simply bottle the stuff, inventors had to meet the technological challenge of designing devices that would put radioactivity back into water that had "wilted."

They quickly succeeded. The biggest seller was the Radium Ore Revigator, a jar lined with radium-containing ore that would create radon as it decayed. The radon was then absorbed in the water inside the jar, which was intended for drinking.

The San Francisco-based company's sales pitch was simple. The water being consumed by virtually all Americans had lost its vitality and was "tired and wilted." Its advertising claimed that most illnesses arose because "radioactivity has been lost from our daily supply of drinking water."

Hundreds of thousands of Revigators were sold. "The millions of tiny rays that are continuously given off by this ore penetrate the water and form this great Health Element—Radio-Activity," read a brochure for the product during its heyday in the 1920s. "All the next day the family is provided with two gallons of real, healthful radioactive water. Nature's way to health."

The beginning of the end came on March 30, 1932. Eben M. Byers, a national amateur golf champion in 1906 and founder of one of the world's largest steel companies, injured his arm during a party after a Harvard-Yale football game in 1928 and, at the advice of his doctor, started what became a two-year, daily habit of downing three bottles of Radithor, one of the most popular radium products of its time.

A dollar-a-bottle concoction of distilled water and two kinds of radium, Radithor sold an estimated forty thousand bottles worldwide in just five years beginning in 1925. Radithor's maker, Bailey Radium Labs, offered a thousand-dollar reward to anyone who could prove that it contained less than the amount of radium they claimed.

Like the radium suppositories, the drink was touted as a sexual enhancer and as a cure for lack of energy in general. For Byers, it was much, much more.

When his teeth started falling out in 1930, he quit his daily habit. Before he died, at age fifty-one on March 30, 1932, he was covered with sores. Because ingested radium tends to gravitate toward the bones, which it then dissolves, he had holes in his skull and much of his upper and lower jaws had rotted away. He weighed just ninety-two pounds.

Byers's death at Doctors Hospital in New York City was front-page news, inspiring tighter regulation of radioactive products and pretty much killing the mass appeal of radium. The *Wall Street Journal* summed it up in a famous headline: "The Radium Water Worked Fine Until His Jaw Came Off."

Byers's remains were exhumed by researchers from the Massachusetts Institute of Technology several decades after his death. Like Curie's notebooks, his skeleton was still radioactive.

Radithor's inventor, William Bailey, died of bladder cancer at the age of sixty-four.

BUT, AS MOST OF US have noticed from time to time, it's hard to keep a good gas down.

Japan—and especially its already bubbling bathing industry—weren't immune from the craze. In the 1920s and 30s, signs touting the radon content of hot springs went up all over the country, and Japanese inventors, though not quite as prolific as their Western counterparts, went about invigorating all kinds of gadgets and health enhancers with radiation's magic glow.

Most are now buried in history's trash heap. But in a testament to the staying power of the craze, two of Japan's most famous additions to the

xxvii

radioactive pharmacy came well after the boom had died down just about everywhere else—even after the country's perception of radiation had been forever changed by Hiroshima and Nagasaki, and as Japanese moviegoers were watching Godzilla, the ultimate downside of radiation therapy, smash his way through Tokyo.

Japan's big contribution was in the field of radiation-enhanced smoking. One, from the 1960s, was called the NICO Clean™ Tobacco Card, a small sheet of metal about the size of a credit card. One side contained low-grade uranium ore, and the card was intended to be slipped into the cellophane cover of a pack of cigarettes. After about twenty minutes, the radiation from the plate, according to its manufacturers, would lower tar and nicotine by an average of 17 percent, reduce the poisonous gas toluene by 50 percent, and "produce milder smoking with no sacrifice in taste."

The second, the Nicotine Alkaloid Control® Plate, was basically a follow-up to the NICO plate. It came out in the 1990s, with the promise that "ions emitted from natural ore denature and reduce nicotine, tar and harmful gas without affecting the original tobacco taste." It was patented in Japan, Italy and the U.S., and though its uranium concentration fell below the regulations of the U.S. Nuclear Regulatory Commission, its maker apparently decided not to market it in America.

Though the more-flamboyant radium gimmicks have faded away, radon spas continue to draw tens of thousands of visitors each year across Europe, Russia and even in the officially radiophobic United States.

In Germany, where the government is relatively permissive toward alternative medicine, radon inhalation and bathing are conducted under the supervision of doctors and are often covered by health insurance. The top-end spas, like Bad Schlema and Bavaria's Sibyllenbad, are elegant, scientific, and frequented not as much by hedonism-driven tourists—as is the case with Misasa—but by the well-to-do, seriously seeking a cure to ailments such as arthritis and asthma. Stays are often several weeks long.

In the Czech Republic, radon treatment is seen as entirely mainstream. At the Radium Palace, an art nouveau sanatorium on the southern slopes of the Ore Mountains, where Marie Curie obtained the uranium from which she isolated radium, patients must have a doctor's recommendation and show their medical records before they are allowed to partake. They are carefully monitored and receive controlled doses of radon.

By contrast, the American situation is very wild, wild west. Some of the best-known facilities in the United States are found in rural Montana, which is home to several converted uranium mineshafts now used as inhalation tunnels. With a rustic appeal, the Free Enterprise, Merry Widow, Earth Angel, and Sunshine mines have recently been undergoing something of a rebirth, and, for bucking the EPA's anti-radon rhetoric, have been the focus of the media spotlight.

But they are a far cry from the luxury of Misasa or the European spas. With little money and no government support, the mines tend to be pretty basic. The trickle of visitors, often middle-class retirees, takes its radon in the shafts, generally in semi-furnished rooms, on couches or at card tables.

It's also a patient-heal-thyself sort of deal. "Though not a state law, it is suggested that children under eighteen years of age obtain a written prescription by a licensed doctor before visiting," the mine states on its Web site. "It is our opinion that visiting during pregnancy is perfectly safe, however if in doubt, do not visit until the first trimester has passed."

The popular appeal of radon spas is causing the scientific community to finally take notice. The potential of radium has long been understood by physicians, but usually in the sense that, "If it doesn't kill you, it will make you stronger."

Killing is, after all, its main use. High doses of radium, used in radiation therapy, are a major tool in the fight against cancer. Employing a variety of increasingly sophisticated techniques, oncologists direct it to the cancerous area and then let its deadly radiation kill the cells around it, both cancerous and healthy.

But researchers over the past two decades have begun to see less-toxic possibilities for radon. Though still a rather limited cadre in the mainstream of science and medicine, radon's supporters claim that numerous studies, along with the long history of reported cures at radon spas, indicate radon treatments, either through inhalation or immersion in baths, have a demonstrated beneficial effect on such ailments as arthritis, chronic pain, and even some forms of cancer.

Their basic premise is fairly simple. First, they say, one cannot assume that because something is poisonous in high doses it will also be poisonous in small amounts. Alcohol and caffeine are good examples. Though they can have positive effects in moderation, both can kill if taken in excess. So can water, for that matter.

And second, it is well established that the stimulus provided to the immune system by a small intrusion of something nasty can at times prove to be a good thing. This is why so many of us have had our shots. Hair of the dog.

But what about radiation? The generally accepted position on radiation in the scientific community is known as the linear no-threshold model, which holds that it is prudent to assume radiation is a carcinogen in any dose level. That's why the EPA warns against any exposure.

This assumption is based in large part on the results of the cohort study on the Hiroshima and Nagasaki survivors—Dr. Waldren's research—that suggests a fairly clear correlation between high-dose exposure and cancer.

There isn't much else to go on. Ethical considerations pretty much rule out experiments on humans, although Three Mile Island and Chernobyl survivors have also provided some clues to the dose-cancer link.

The weak spot in the no-dose-is-safe assumption is that there is very little data regarding low-dose radiation. In the 1980s, T.D. Luckey, professor emeritus at the University of Missouri, examined that weakness, then made the radical claim that, the obvious dangers of high dosage notwithstanding, low-dose irradiation can actually be beneficial.

Research now suggests low-level radiation may increase the production of proteins involved in repairing DNA, stimulate the immune system, and even suppress certain kinds of cancer. Luckey's theory, called radiation hormesis, has been accepted as dogma in Misasa; the town outlines the idea in glowing terms in many of its official brochures and on the village Web site, and further notes a study by Japanese researchers that showed lung cancer in the village was about 50 percent of the level found in a lower-radon control area.

"Everyone is talking about it!" the site gushes. "The wonders of our fountain of youth have been proven."

Well, not quite. There are many who still write off hormesis as wishful thinking—but flawed science. And no one has yet established a clear limit for low-dose radiation treatment beyond which the dangers start.

Even so, hormesis has put some of the old spark back into the radioactive waters. "Seven years ago hormesis would not find its way into an informal conversation among toxicologists. Now, we not only know that it exists, but accept its dominance over other models," Edward Calabrese and Linda Baldwin of the University of Massachusetts, Amherst, wrote in the journal *Nature* in February 2003. "The implications are enormous."

THE OFUNA RADON HOT Springs are a working man's—or, more accurately, a budget-conscious retiree's—version of Ohashi's Misasa inn. Hidden away in a shady hillside near an ancient Buddhist temple in a Tokyo suburb, the bathhouse, like dozens of others in the capital area, was built in the 1920s, when Japan was caught up with the rest of the industrialized world in the radium boom.

At the height of the fad, some seventy radium bathhouses and hot springs competed for the attentions of local residents in one small neighborhood between Yokohama and Tokyo. Today, only one—the Tsunashima Radium Hot Springs—is left.

Ofuna's better days are also almost certainly behind it. Rundown and tacky—souvenirs include "radon muffins"—the bathhouse has none of Misasa's elegance, or history. Nor do its waters naturally bubble up from the ground. The radon in its "medicinal healing room" is infused into the bath with somewhat mysterious "radon-producing machines."

Though a few times more expensive than the average public bath, Ofuna is like an old folks' activity center. After bathing, or instead of it, the guests join in bingo games, karaoke sing-alongs and group dances on a stage in front of the dining area, which is all low tables and tatami mats. There are rooms for watching TV or simply napping with no fear of interruption. Shuttle buses pick up guests at the nearest train station, and drop them off again afterward. Even on weekdays, the hot springs are busy, if not over-flowing.

Just how much radon is actually in the bath is also a mystery. I was politely ushered out when I began asking too many questions.

The Japanese government takes a low-key approach to radon's dangers, and there is little effort made to publicize studies that suggest it is better avoided than actively sought out. Few of the regulars know of radon's bad reputation abroad. If they did, most wouldn't care. Perhaps even more than in Misasa, Ofuna's clientele are a faithful lot.

"All I know is that it definitely makes me feel better," said Masako Okubo, a sprightly seventy-five-year-old grandmother who has been dousing herself in Ofuna's waters twice a week for six years, when I mentioned the American EPA's warnings. "My shoulders feel much better after I bathe here." Okubo admitted radon may not be the main reason why bathing here perks her up, however.

"I'm no doctor, but I know this place is good for me," Okubo told me as she ate her lunch one afternoon. Other than the waitresses, I was the only person under the age of sixty in the cafeteria, and possibly in the whole building.

"If nothing else, it's relaxing," she said, her short black-and gray-hair sporting streaks of blue, as is the fashion for older ladies in this country.

"It's a social thing. I like the people here," she said between chopsticks full of rice and shrimp tempura. "Maybe that's more important than all the radon."

But others give clear credit to the waters. When Hatsu Motegi was eighty-six, her leg began to hurt so badly that she couldn't walk. She went to a doctor, who began treating her and prescribing painkillers. For two months, she continued under his care, but made no progress.

"It got very disturbing. Then a friend suggested we come here," Motegi's daughter, an Ofuna devotee herself, told me. "After just a couple of visits, she was walking again. That was two years ago. We've kept coming every few months since."

xxviii

IX

DIRTY WATER

A visit to Soapland, where cleanliness isn't next to godliness.
How some bathhouses got nasty
in the days of the samurai and have since evolved
into a mainstay of Japan's sex industry.

IT'S THREE O'CLOCK on a Wednesday afternoon, and time for Norika to set up for work. She changes out of her street clothes and into a silky white, full-length gown, checks to see that there are enough condoms on a little stand by the bed, and then has one last smoke as she begins drawing the bath.

Her room at the end of a long hall, eight doors down from the parlor where the day's first wave of guests await, is basically as she left it the last time she was on duty a couple of days before. There is a tiny desk covered with cosmetics, a half-empty bottle of mineral water, and a basket filled with about a dozen packs of cigarettes, each a different brand. On the pink carpet is a knee-high table, with more cigarettes, more condoms, a laminated menu listing several drinks. A box of tissues. Against the wall, the small bed is wrapped in a dark gray blanket, tightly enough to make a boot camp drill sergeant proud.

As I take off my shoes at the doorway and step inside, it strikes me that this half of the room is pretty much like any other cramped, cluttered Tokyo apartment. "Cozy" is definitely not the right word, though it does have a very lived-in feel to it. In a vague sort of way, it takes me back to my college days.

The other half, however, is a bit of a departure.

A half-step down from the carpeted floor, the tile-covered bathing area begins. A full-size tub takes up one side. A light-brown plastic sauna—the old box kind, in which you are enclosed with only your head sticking out—fills the other corner.

Lotions and soaps are lined up on the floor in between. There is an oddly shaped plastic stool of a variety you're not likely to see at home. And over it all, propped up against the wall, looms a huge silvery air mattress.

Like millions of Japanese women, Norika is a fan of Hello Kitty, and she has decorated her room with the ubiquitous cartoon cat. Kitty dolls cover her desk and sit smiling on her table. A Kitty towel hangs over the door, blocking the window onto the hallway that is required by law. She stubs out her smoke in a Kitty ashtray, and as she talks she fiddles with a Kitty pouch filled with yet more condoms.

"It has kind of taken on a life of its own," she told me, a bit embarrassed. "I brought some Kitty things in, and then my clients started giving me Kitty presents. Now I have more Kitty than I know what to do with."

She excuses herself for a moment, turns on a Mary J. Blige CD and adjusts the volume so that it is just loud enough to allow us to talk but also provide a solid wall of background noise to drown out the occasional intrusions of chatter from the hallway and dull, thumping sounds from the adjacent room.

"I like to add my own touch, with Kitty and the music and stuff," she says as she sits barefoot on the floor by the table. "It makes things more pleasant, you know?"

Norika is taller than average, but not quite fashion-model height. Her hair, dyed light brown, falls past her bare shoulders. She has big eyes, but, other than mascara, is wearing no makeup. Quite deliberately, her full body is accentuated by the clingy gown, which is cut low at the chest.

Norika, by the way, isn't her real name. Like the other women where she works, she uses a "stage" name given her by the brothel manager. She asked that I not use her real name, or even her full working name (she's been given a surname, too). And I was allowed in only after also agreeing to not use the name of the brothel.

Not that Norika or her employers are all that afraid of publicity. She has her own home page. As does her employer, whose Web site features glossy photos of Norika and all the other girls, detailed descriptions of what to expect, and contact numbers for making reservations. Neither, however, wants the authorities to know they have talked to an outsider.

"That's not the kind of attention we like," the manager, a husky man with a tightly curled haircut and the raspy voice of a chain smoker, told me before showing me to the waiting room. "We prefer a low profile."

At thirty-two, Norika has been doing this longer than most. When she was in high school, looking for a quick way to make money to buy clothes and accessories, she got herself into what is euphemistically known as *enjo kosai*, a phrase coined in the 1980s that translates literally into "assistance dating." It's an unnaturally formal, academic-sounding term—*enjo,* which means "assistance," is more comfortably applied to such concepts as foreign aid than teenage prostitution.

But there was no higher purpose to what Norika was doing. It was prostitution, pure and simple. Her dates were usually middle-age men who would take her to "love hotels," where rooms can be rented for a couple of hours or for the whole night. She came out a hundred dollars or so richer.

After her parents' divorce she left school and her native Osaka to follow her boyfriend to Tokyo. That didn't work out, and she once again found herself in need of an income. She started working in hostess bars, pouring drinks and providing conversation and a young body for businessmen to paw in the after-hours. The money was good, she said, but not all that great. Moreover, she was never good at planning ahead and found it hard to build up any savings or to find a decent apartment that would accept a young woman in the *mizu shobai*, or "water business," as the world of nightlife is called.

Living out of a weekly hotel, she decided to start turning tricks on the side. Before long, she just quit the hostessing part altogether. "I got an early start selling my body, so by that time I didn't have much resistance to the idea," she said. "I did basically everything: S/M clubs, massage parlors, the works."

Then, at the ripe age of twenty, she discovered Soapland.

YOSHIWARA IS ONE OF Tokyo's most famous districts. It's got centuries of colorful history. Books have been written and movies have been made about the lives of its inhabitants.

But officially it doesn't exist. It has been erased from the maps. Redistricted. Renamed.

By design, Yoshiwara is out of the way. And it always has been. Unless you have some specific business in Yoshiwara (and Yoshiwara is pretty much a one-business place), it's just not a neighborhood you would ever go to, or even pass through.

Though Tokyo has one of the best subway networks in the world, and though Yoshiwara is in a heavily populated district in Tokyo proper, it's a hike from just about anywhere. There are two train stations that serve the area, but neither is within easy walking distance.

For most people in Tokyo, Yoshiwara is about as out of sight, out of mind as a place could possibly get. As I was planning my own cross-town trip there, I quickly discovered that aside from those associated by their work with the place, or those who had written about or studied it, no one I knew had ever actually gone.

It was almost like it didn't really exist. Like it was just another of those hot-summer-night male fantasies, or some sort of eerie urban mirage.

The thing is, it most certainly does exist. And it has, in one form or another, been there, right in the same spot, for about four hundred years, making its urban-legend aspect seem even weirder.

But Yoshiwara was about to become real for me. After a couple decades in Tokyo, for the first time I did have business in Yoshiwara. I was going to Soapland.

So, after getting my bearings and hurrying away from a throng of street-walkers outside the wrong end of the station, I found my way to the proper exit, where I lined up with about a dozen young women on their way to work and, like everyone else, hopped in a taxi. Almost without even need-ing to ask, the driver knew exactly where I was going. And, despite the paucity of maps, there was no mistaking it when we arrived.

As you have likely guessed by now, Yoshiwara is Tokyo's premier red light district, and this being Japan, it has a lot to do with baths.

The district is literally wall-to-wall brothels, dozens and dozens of them, for about four full city blocks. There are no vacant lots. And thanks to increasingly picky zoning laws, property is so precious here that it would be hard for a skinny cat to squeeze its way through what little unused space remains between most of the brothels.

I got out near one of the two police stations that mark the outer corners of the district and—it was my first time, after all—probably gawked a bit as I walked the rest of the way.

Not everything was unexpected. As in just about every red light district the world over, outside each brothel stood at least one man in a dark suit who touted the wonders of the harems that awaited upstairs, or greeted the cars of newly arriving customers.

There was lots of neon, announcing brothels bearing such names as the New Sunflower, Satin Doll, Last Scene, the Blue Chateau. One had a sort of turn-of-the-century French look. Another had a classically Japanese exterior, all dark wood and windowless. There were decorative balconies, towering façades. Chrome and marble were favored materials, and inside each doorway stood big, colorful flower arrangements.

None of it really worked.

Yoshiwara isn't classy. It's expensive. It *can* be exclusive—many of the brothels, for example, won't allow foreigners inside. But the area comes across as gaudy, and a little bit weary and unrooted. False, pretentious. Tawdry, I guess. What little space there was that wasn't devoted to the brothels themselves was given over to related endeavors.

On my little walk, I passed a couple of coffee shops where the uninitiated can get free advice on where to go—the brothels themselves cover the costs. I saw a few expensive and very well-stocked lingerie shops, and a couple of short-term apartments for the women who choose—or are forced by their employers—to live nearby.

But, along with all of its red-light cliches, Yoshiwara does have a certain character of its own. For example, it doesn't feel the least bit dangerous. There are no streetwalkers here, no pimps, no cheap hotels—though all of those things can be found alongside the railroad tracks near one of the train stations, which I discovered earlier when I got out at the wrong exit and, a couple of blocks later, found myself on a side street swarming with Chinese prostitutes.

But because most customers in Yoshiwara itself are willing to pay for privacy, there aren't many people on its streets. Most of the business here is done by appointment, with dark limousines shuffling back and forth between the brothels and the local train stations, picking up customers and dropping them off right at the door.

When I arrived at Norika's, I was greeted by two smiling men and the customary sign listing the prices for all to see.

There are generally three categories of Soapland brothels in Yoshiwara. The cheapest start at about ¥10,000 for an hour or so. Next up, the "brothels for the masses," which begin at around twice that. Anything over ¥40,000 is considered high-class.

But what the signs say the fees are for is what really makes Yoshiwara unique. What you pay for in Yoshiwara—at first, at least—is a bath.

And you do, in fact, get one.

BACK IN NORIKA'S ROOM, I sat self-consciously and uncomfortably on the big mattress as she pulled up her gown and squatted by the shower nozzle to mix up a bowlful of lotion, kneading it into a stream of hot water until it had the proper consistency. When it was just right, she pulled out her hand to create a long trail of transparent gook.

"I get real slippery when I put this on," she said. "Guys seem to like that."

What happens in the rooms of Soapland is highly ritualized, and it separates these brothels from other sex businesses, even within Japan. What happens here doesn't happen anywhere else in the world.

Norika's clients get one hundred and ten minutes—there are two clocks in her room, one on the desk and one on the table—and though each hostess (in Japanese they are called "soap-*jo*" or soap girls) has a certain amount of freedom to take the lead, the content of the sessions is pretty clear-cut.

A warning to the timid. This is going to get a little graphic. You might want to skip ahead a bit.

"Basically, we do five things," Norika explained. Her sessions begin with sex. "This is usually something you only get at a real high-class club, because it means I am willing to do this before washing the man off," she said. "That is a special service."

After that, she brings her clients to the bathing area, and the washing begins. In keeping with the general Japanese custom, both must wash off before getting in the tub, which by this time is full. So she cleans her clients by hand and tongue, head to toe.

She doesn't use sponges or wash towels.

"That's a no-no. I can't give the impression that I am hesitating, or he might think I see him as too dirty to touch." This, of course, is a key point.

The Soapland concept plays heavily on the Japanese penchant for cleanliness. Soap girls are paid not just to satisfy their client's sexual desires, but to free them of all their dirtiness. Top to bottom, with no hesitation.

Once in the bath, Norika said, she both brushes her client's teeth and provides other services, such as a form of oral sex called the "periscope," which should not demand too much from the reader's imagination to figure out.

When they get out, she puts on the lotion and has the man sit on the stool, which has a slit across the top and is just big enough for her to squeeze her way under. Thus underneath her client, she continues her cleaning. They then lie on the mattress, where she does what is called the *awa odori*, or "bubble dance."

"Actually, we call it the mat dance these days, since we don't use soap to make bubbles anymore," Norika said. "Lotion is much easier on the skin."

This is perhaps the most famous part of the Soapland experience. "It's really vigorous," Norika said. "I'm like a human towel. It's hard to do, and even harder to explain. Some girls pick it up faster, but I would say it took me three years before I felt I could really do it well. I think I'm pretty good at it now."

Suffice it to say, the dance is done horizontally.

These elements—the cleaning, the bath, the stool, the mattress, and sex either before or after—are what defines the Soapland experience.

"My role is to utterly devote myself to him," she said. "I do everything. I am totally at his service."

Technically, the soap girls are self-employed. They rent their rooms— used solely for work; they live elsewhere—from the Soapland owners and pay a fee for the towels and other essentials, such as meals, that they will need during the day. Prostitution laws are skirted because customers pay the Soapland establishments to provide a bath, not sex. And, separately, they pay the soap girls for services provided as, for lack of a better phrase, bathing assistants.

If the soap girl is moved to have sex in the course of their private interaction, well, that's her choice.

As long as she is legally an adult, it's a free world. And the police can go on comfortably doing their paperwork down the street, peacefully oblivious.

THE BATHS OF YOSHIWARA are the direct descendants of the baths of yore. Public bathing in the feudal period was initially a fairly straightforward endeavor. The baths opened in the morning and closed in the evening and offered only a rudimentary sort of service that was, in fact, more like a group sauna than a bath because of the difficulty and expense of filling tubs with hot water.

The bathhouses were dark and dank and prone to chilly breezes. But as the popularity of public bathing grew, and competition increased, things got more attractive.

One of the first big changes in medieval bathing was the addition of rooms upstairs where guests could enjoy a cup of tea after their bath. This led to women being brought in to serve the tea. Then, women were brought into the baths themselves to wash the guests' backs. From there, it was back upstairs again to provide more private services.

By the seventeenth century, the metamorphosis of bathhouse into brothel was complete. The attendants, called *yuna*, or "hot water girls," would wear light cotton robes into the bath to assist bathers in getting clean during the day, then change into more provocative attire after hours, when their duties included providing music, tea, and sex, often in an upstairs lounge area built specially for that purpose. Most of the sento built in the Edo period had a second floor. And most second floors were well used.

Yoshiwara, meanwhile, was developing a life of its own.

Less than twenty years after Edo became the political capital of Japan, the samurai rulers designated Yoshiwara, then little more than a reed bog, as the sole legal zone for prostitution. It was seen as a necessary evil.

From its early days, Edo was a man's city. In 1733, government records indicate that the city had a population of 540,000, all but 200,000 of them men. Add on another 500,000 men in the samurai caste not counted in the population figures—many of them living in the capital away from their families—and you have a decidedly low percentage of available females.

By the time Yoshiwara was established in 1617, brothels had already sprung up all over town. The samurai government, realizing that it wasn't likely to succeed if it tried to ban prostitution altogether, decided that Yoshiwara was far enough out of the way to provide a discreet steam valve for the city's teeming male masses.

It was a decision that stuck. Though the district burned down with much of the rest of old Edo in 1657, it was rebuilt in its present location and prospered famously. At its peak, an estimated three thousand prostitutes worked in Yoshiwara, and some of its brothels—immortalized in countless woodblock prints—were the height of luxury and opulence.

The area has always had a dark side, however. Back then Yoshiwara was surrounded by high walls and a moat, entry restricted to a guarded gate. That wasn't so much to keep tabs on the customers as it was to keep the women, who were allowed to leave only to see the cherry blossoms or to attend to a dying relative, from escaping their imprisonment inside.

And while Yoshiwara was a huge success, the official attempt at keeping prostitution limited to inside its walls was doomed from the start. Along with the bathhouses and various other kinds of dubious tearooms, prostitution flourished along the banks of the Sumida River, where prostitutes carried their own straw mats so that they could set up shop just about anywhere. Deals were made on pleasure boats, even at temple festivals.

Concerned about the impact of unregulated prostitution on public morals, officials tried repeatedly to crack down. Prostitution at the baths was banned after an earthquake devastated the capital in 1703. That obviously didn't work very well, because it had to be banned again in 1841, when the yuna were forced to move into Yoshiwara.

Ever resilient, they adapted, and for the next century the sex trade continued to flourish. With the yuna gone, the banning of mixed bathing in 1890 pretty much finished off the bathhouse as brothel tradition. Public baths were finally coming clean.

But when one door is closed, another is opened.

WE MOVE FORWARD to the year 1951.

Japan is still recovering from its crushing defeat in World War II, its cities still in ashes, its government still controlled by the U.S.-led Occupation, and on the outskirts of the soon-to-be-swanky Ginza shopping district, a massage parlor called the Tokyo Hot Springs creates a sensation by offering Turkish baths—basically those little sauna boxes—in private rooms staffed by Miss Turkeys, pretty young women dressed in short-sleeved white cotton robes and short pants.

Sex isn't on the menu, yet. But the die is cast.

Turkish baths start popping up all over the country, appearing in amusement quarters from Kyushu to Hokkaido. Within two years, there are dozens. Twenty in Tokyo alone. And they are now starting to offer *o-supe*, or special services which involved, well, the use of the hands. By 1956, the services include the use of other body parts as well.

Like their samurai predecessors, the post-Occupation government is by now growing increasingly anxious about the spread of prostitution. But unlike the samurai, they ban it outright. Yoshiwara is shut down. Brothels around the country close. And on March 31, 1958, the red lights went out.

But the Turkish baths survived. Unable to run brothels, Yoshiwara entrepreneurs adopted the Turkish bath system wholesale. The special services are revived, and by 1960 they begin offering sex as well.

Of course, there continue to be some bumps. A water shortage in 1962 forces the baths to close temporarily, and the Tokyo Olympics in 1964 bring increased pressure from the authorities. Crimes involving gangsters also dog the new businesses, with shootings generating both headlines in the tabloid press and increased pressure from the police and anti-prostitution activists.

But by the 1970s there are more than a thousand Turkish baths across the country, and more than two hundred in Tokyo alone—a quarter of them in Yoshiwara. And just like their feudal ancestors, the postwar entrepreneurs used innovation to set themselves apart from the crowd.

While the rest of Japan was enjoying the Olympics, Turkish bath connoisseurs were getting their first taste of the air mattress at Benten in Tokyo's Ueno district. The use of body oils and lotions was started at Utamaro in 1967, a year many in the business consider the golden age of assisted bathing. Yoshiwara's trademark bath stools were first brought out in Azuma in 1970. And the bubble dance was pretty well established in Yoshiwara by 1978.

Trouble was brewing, however. There is some debate over what exactly went wrong. But the most often-told version is that by the early 1980s, when millions of men were visiting Turkish baths each year, the Turkish Embassy in Tokyo began receiving phone calls from prospective "customers" inquiring about rates and reservations.

There may, or may not, have actually been a Turkish bath that went by the name the Turkish Embassy. Unfortunately, that's an element of the story that I have never been able to confirm. It sounds very plausible, but some say it is an urban legend.

Be that as it may. Protests from Turkish officials over the insult to their national pride posed by having their country's name sullied as a synonym for sex houses (from the 1960s on, "Turkish girl" had also become the euphemism for prostitute) grew so loud that the fracas threatened to become an all-out diplomatic battle. So, in 1985, the 110-member trade association of Turkish bathhouse owners in Tokyo decided to hold a nationwide contest to find a new name.

It was an inspired idea. Some 2,200 suggestions were submitted from the general public, and the press conference to announce the new name was attended not only by representatives of the Turkish Embassy (the real one) but also by virtually all of Japan's major media.

The result, trumpeted across headlines nationwide the following day: "Soapland." It was the brainchild of Seiichi Ishida, a Tokyo office worker.

Overnight, the word "Turkey" vanished from the lexicon of Japan's sex industry. But Soapland's roots have not completely disappeared. Though she says she has never used it, there remains that little box sauna—a Turkish bath—in the corner of Norika's room, and countless rooms like it across the country.

Traditions die hard.

TODAY, BUSINESS IN SOAPLAND is probably as good as it's ever been. Though I went to see Norika on a weekday afternoon, the waiting room (replete with the ubiquitous flower arrangement, the ever-smiling waiters in tuxedos, and a huge flat-screen television) was nearly full. It was also, I am told, full of a pretty representative bunch of the clientele.

There was a college student with a backpack. A chubby, middle-age office worker in suit and tie, briefcase in hand. Another, more dapper, middle-age man in a turtleneck and tweed jacket. A couple of thirtysomething guys in baseball caps, their faces buried in tabloids.

On an average day, Norika said, she will see three men. Five is her limit, mainly because the bubble dance takes too much out of her. "It gets really busy around New Year," she said. "April is busy, too."

Japan's sex trade in general is booming. Estimates of the industry are by nature only ballpark figures, but head upward of two to three trillion yen a year. Norika estimated her monthly income, after expenses, at about ¥700,000, fairly typical for a soap girl but well over the average a women her age could expect to make on the more conventional job market.

She has a relatively free schedule as well. She works two days, then takes two days off. And her hours are pretty much set by law. "Officially, we are required to close shop at midnight," she said. "But if I'm with a guy who has just come in, I may stay a bit later."

Soapland is by no means the only choice out there. "Pink salons" specialize in oral sex. "Delivery Health" refers to call girls who deliver themselves to wherever her customer may desire. On the low end there are fashion massages, peep shows with extras, cabarets, you name it. The high end gravitates more toward specialty fetishes, more personalized services, higher quality.

Soapland falls into the high end. And, surely, at several hundred dollars an hour, it isn't cheap. But because it is closer to being on the up-and-up than most other varieties of pay sex, it is also relatively safe. The yakuza underworld reaps significant profits from the establishments in the form of protection money and exorbitant fees charged for renting towels and other supplies. But violence and blatant rip-offs are uncommon.

For clients, the gangster connection generally remains in the shadows. The service is painstakingly polite and prices generally include the little extras, such as cigarettes and drinks, that are used in more dubious places to run up a huge bill. That is, in fact, one of the main attractions of Soapland. You know what you're getting into.

"There really is no competition for the Soaplands," said Chisato Kakinuma, a freelance writer and photographer who has specialized in covering the sex trade for decades. "They are clean, basically legal, and the women have regular health checks. Plus, it's a specialty all of its own."

Kakinuma said Soapland is also a safer world for the women than most other options in the industry. In lower-class brothels, where the women work directly for pimps, there is a much higher likelihood of physical abuse. The rise of the delivery health agencies, which took off in the late 1990s after a crackdown forced sex industry entrepreneurs to seek new loopholes, also has meant increased risks for the women involved.

"If it weren't for the money, I wouldn't be doing this at all," Norika said. "But this is also a pretty comfortable place to be working. We are expensive. The owners of this place need us to be happy. So they treat us well."

She didn't have much to say about the men who come to her. "I suppose it just feels good to be cleaned by someone," she said with a shrug. "It's a very Japanese thing, I think. Japanese men kind of have a thing about that."

And of herself?

"I guess it does require some ability to just not think about my job too deeply," she said, crushing out another cigarette and straightening the front of her gown. "But I don't have to do this. I'm here because I choose to be. I could never work a regular nine-to-five job. I want to keep doing this as long as I can bring in the customers.

"I figure I still have a few more years."

She admitted that the concept of Soapland, and the whole dirty/clean fetish, is an especially taxing one.

"It really can take its toll. If you think about it too much, it can really mess you up," she said. "I've seen a lot of the girls come apart. Get depressed or get involved in bad things just trying to distract themselves.

"I mean, we are expected to do things that are pretty demeaning, things that might be okay with a partner you love but are pretty hard to do with just anybody."

Still, Norika said that compared to the other sex businesses she's been in, Soapland has the advantage of allowing her to at least make sure that her customers are clean.

"Having a bath right there can actually be quite a relief sometimes," she said.

X

SEEKING THE ESSENCE

Additives, the Buddhist water goddess,
Shinto's cleansing fetish,
and how scientists are sucking the water out of the bath
in search of its true essence

I ENJOY CORRUPTING the waters of my bath.

I am corrupting my latest tubful right now, soaking not merely in hot water, but in *enhanced* hot water. Tonight's enhancement is a fizzy lozenge called "Bub," which I tossed into the tub a few minutes before hopping in myself, making it effervesce quite satisfactorily and turn a military green. This particular variety of Bub, Bub-J, was designed to produce the effect of a forest. In bath logic, that apparently involves being heavily perfumed with a decidedly non-woodsy, and, to my nose anyway, kind of prissy, scent. But the package also claims that Bub-J will help me absorb more heat from my bath, ease my nagging fatigue, and fix that stiff neck of mine.

Actually, the Japanese don't say stiff neck. They say "stiff shoulders." But it's the same thing.

There are a gazillion Bubs on the market here. First, you've got your basic enhancers, the lozenges that fizzle up and turn the bath both fragrant and colorful. There are your simple salts and powders and milks. For the hardcore bath enthusiast, there are ion-altering contraptions and filters of every stripe. Then there are the hot springs essences. My neighborhood drugstore, like every drugstore in the country, has a whole section devoted to this stuff.

Bath salts and powders of all kinds are generally called *nyuyokuzai*—very roughly, "medicine for the water." There is a promise here of relief. This is a realm that welcomes the old and the tired. The haggard housewife. The white-collar worker making his way home after a long day manning the desk. The section devoted to bubble baths and other concoctions more self-consciously aimed at tickling the fancy of young single women—the demographic so zealously courted for everything else—is, for these purposes, not that important.

People over the age of twenty-six rule these waters. So here goes another confession: I, a middle-age straight white male, hang out in the bath aisle of my local drugstore more than is required by mere pragmatic necessity. What can I say? People like me fit in here. Like me, just about everybody in Japan is over the age of twenty-six these days, and by the middle of the century one-third will be over sixty-five. The shelves here are dedicated to us, the aging masses, and the wholly Japanese love for—and almost religious belief in—the powers of bathing.

For me, browsing through the bath powders in the drugstore is like killing time in the travel corner of a bookstore. Or maybe the travel corner of a Christian bookstore. Though the various kinds of Bub are location-neutral, most bathwater additives claim to reproduce miraculous effects of specific, and often exclusive or especially out-of-the-way, hot springs.

Thanks to my neighborhood drugstore, I can sample the waters of several dozen of the best resorts in the country, from northern Hokkaido's

Noboribetsu to Beppu on the southern isle of Kyushu, by simply mixing the packets of these magical powdered essences into my tap water.

This always struck me as ironic. I envision white-coated researchers hard at work in their laboratories across the country, toiling day after day to find the essence of the perfect bath—by sucking the wetness out of the water.

This pursuit is, however, a well-established tradition. Hot springs often contain what is euphemistically called *oyu no hana*, or bath flowers. Put in simple terms, these flowers are clumps of coagulated crap that have bubbled up with the mineral water and are now contentedly floating around in it.

In some baths, it can be quite a distraction. But, for those in the know, the presence of bath flowers is considered to be a sign of both authenticity and potency. I personally appreciate how they solve an old public bathing conundrum by offering me something to do with my hands: swish them away or squish them between my fingers.

For the common bathers who, unlike the samurai and aristocratic nobility, are not rich enough to have the waters delivered to their estates, dried bath flowers have been hawked at hot springs since feudal times. Put into neat bags, the dried and sifted flowers are renamed and sold as *onsen no moto*, or hot springs essence. Most major resorts still offer them.

But the essence industry has come a long way since the samurai days. Tsumura & Co., a leading producer of bath essence, has turned the trade into a fine science. The company, one of Japan's largest herbal pharmaceutical producers, boasts of the dedication of its scientists to the discovery of new and improved uses of natural remedies based on holistic medicine and the ancient Chinese pharmacopoeia known in Japan as *kanpo*.

Tsumura was founded in Tokyo in 1893 to market a concoction called *Chujo-to*, a cure for what the company gently calls "women's complaints." But, according to the company's 2003 annual report, the firm's creators soon realized that the same herbal cure when mixed with water "made a refreshing and invigorating bath additive."

Today, Tsumura controls roughly a quarter of the bath additive market in Japan, to the tune of around ¥13 billion, around $110 million. It also continues to sell Chujo-to as a tea that promotes relaxation and, here we go again, "helps regulate various body functions that are unique to women."

It's quite a mixture, containing White Peony Root, Japanese Angelica Root, Cinnamon Bark, Cnidium Rhizome, Tree Peony Bark, Polyporus Sclerotium, Southern Tsangshu Rhizome, Rehmannia Root, Bitter Orange Peel, Licorice Root, Nut Grass Rhizome, Peach Kernel, Chinese Goldthread Rhizome, Ginger Rhizome, Clove Floral Bud, and Oriental Ginseng Root.

My point is that these people take their business seriously. But they say it best: "If we can make proper use of the results of such researches and the knowledge of traditional hot springs cures," they assure prospective customers, "we can expect wonderful benefits from bathing in terms of maintaining and advancing mental and physical health and beauty, curing disease and rehabilitation." In its effort to spread the word, Tsumura maintains a highly entertaining Web site, in Japanese and English, that explains everything from how to take a bath *à la Japonaise* to the medical basis for bathing's physical benefits to a goal-specific table that lists different ways to achieve different "results" from bathing.

Feeding the Japanese bath enthusiasts' subconscious need to be scientifically validated (as opposed to being just a bunch of scintillation-seeking hedonists), this part of the site can get rather arcane, especially when it delves into the roles of the sympathetic and parasympathetic nerve systems.

Don't feel left out if your gross anatomy isn't what it used to be. I had to look it up myself. Just think of it this way. The sympathetic nerve system originates in the middle of the spinal chord and prepares the body for "fight or flight"-style activity, while the parasympathetic system extends from the upper and lower spine and serves to calm one down to "rest and digest" after the fight response is no longer needed.

When preparing for work, the Tsumura bath doctors advise, a quick, hot bath is best because it will stimulate the sympathetic nerves to "dominate and increase the tension of mind and body." Inducing peaceful sleep or relieving stress, meanwhile, is best accomplished by a long, lukewarm soak, which prompts the parasympethetic system "to dominate and tranquilize mind and body." The same is recommended for "worming the body" [sic].

Tsumura's most popular product is its "Japan's Famous Hot Springs" line, a series of powder packets which, when put in bathwater, "replicate the color and ion composition of one of Japan's most renowned naturally medicinal hot springs" and allow bathers to "experience the rejuvenating effects and tranquil natural ambience of Japan's legendary mineral spas—*all in the comfort of your home.*"

I love the concept. So many different journeys awaiting you right there in the bath, the room in the home where the imagination is most ready to take flight in so many different, delicious directions.

Of course, a good imagination is required. The packets and lozenges, while approximating certain aspects of their stated models, create a bath that is about as close to the real resorts as the descriptions in Jules Vernes's novel were to the real center of the Earth.

As I soak in the replicated waters of Izu, I accept that, were this the real deal, I would not be immersed in a milky pink mixture with a smell of flowers and sweetness. Izu, being volcanic and sulfuric, smells more like flatulence. But it's the thought that counts, at least for me.

Not all would agree. There is a strong element that takes its water much more seriously.

MASARU EMOTO, founder of the International Hado Movement, is the Japanese guru of water. In his books, his Web site, and his travels, he tells of how all of us are constantly interacting with water, badly mostly, and how we really need to stop mucking it up. We are turning our water ugly with our bad vibes, setting ourselves up for the kind of devastation that only some really, really pissed-off water can wreak.

We're talking Noah here. The signs are everywhere. The tsunami that ravished southern Asia just after Christmas in 2004, washing away more than one hundred thousand people. The hurricane that inundated New Orleans the following summer, leaving hundreds of thousands homeless. If we're not careful, Emoto tells us, the whole Earth could be headed down the road to Atlantis.

Emoto's theory, first put forth in a couple of bestselling books published amid the deluge of New Age philosophizing at the start of the new millennium, is fairly easy to grasp.

He believes that our thoughts can alter the structure of the water molecules around us, and as proof he offers high-speed photos of water crystals taken at the instant they froze under various influences, ranging from the sweet harmonies of Mozart (which create a beautifully intricate snowflake pattern) to the lyrics of rapper Eminem's "You Make Me Sick" (which turn a microscopic drip of water into what appears to be a blob of brown barf).

Most water, Emoto argues, has lost its all-important hexagonal shape due to distillation, pollution, and bad vibrations. But water that still has its hexagonal structure, like the water that shapes snowflakes, "forms an organized crystalline matrix with properties that are different from ordinary water." Among those properties, not surprisingly, is the power to heal. Even less surprisingly, Emoto has packaged the stuff, which he calls Indigo Water and sells on his Web site. Along with bottles to put it in. And posters of his favorite water crystals. And happy little stickers to perk up the H_2O coming out of your faucets.

"Put a glass of water on a table in your kitchen, dining room, or private room," Emoto implores his followers. "Tell the water, 'I love you,' and 'Thank you,' gently. At the same time, briefly visualize that all the water on Earth is connected. You can do this with your children, family members, and friends. Your love and thanks will be sent out to all the water on Earth through the water in the glass."

But Emoto says that what he is concerned about isn't science, or profits. He wants to do something about all that delinquent water out there, going bad as it awaits a few kind words as evidence that somebody actually cares.

Emoto claims to have sold several hundred thousand copies of his books, which have been published in Japanese and English. But he admits that only a few dozen people turned up on July 24, 2005, for his "Third World Day of Love and Thanks to Water" at a public hall in, of all places, Eschen, Liechtenstein.

Well, these things take time.

IT'S HARD TO THINK of water as just water.

We either ignore it, taking it for granted as we splash it on our faces or flush it down the toilet, or we exalt it, swirling it into the stuff of myth and instilling it with all kinds of mystical wonders.

Emoto is hardly original in his water worship. The faithful of almost every religion give water a special place. The Catholics have their holy water. The Baptists have their baptisms. The Hindus have the Ganges River. The birth of Sakyamuni Buddha some 2,500 years ago is marked around the globe each May by dousing his statues in ladlefuls of water and flower petals, a recreation of the bath the baby Buddha is believed to have been given by the Nine Heavenly Dragons.

Quacks love the stuff even more. There's pi water. Primodial dew. Magnetic mugs that restore water's proper structure and bring it back to "life." Water altered by advanced quantum physics so that it is less slimy. (Finally! A practical use for quantum phsysics!) Clustered water, energized water, photon water.

Even scientists, who tend to be a fairly dry bunch, admit water is a special substance. Of the 15 million or so known chemical substances, it's the only one that has a solid form that is less dense than its liquid form. Ask your bartender. Ice floats. Water really shouldn't be a liquid at the temperature range that is so convenient for us humans, anyway. If it were like most other chemical substances with a similarly low molecular weight, it would be a gas at room temperature. It should boil and freeze at much lower temperatures than it does. Moreover, it takes a lot of energy to heat water, and then it retains heat for a very long time, sort of like snuggly wrapped baked potatoes.

This is a good thing. Because water covers 70 percent of the Earth's surface, this property is an essential factor enabling life on this planet—since it requires a lot of energy to heat water, and since water tends to cool only gradually, water stabilizes the climate. Of course, water's propensity to retain heat makes baths a lot more pleasant as well.

But the crown jewel of water's properties is that water is wet.

Science offers a (sorry again) solid, though rather involved, explanation. Just as metal seems to shimmer because of an ongoing molecular reaction with photons, water is wet because it is in a constant state of flux. Due to a phenomenon known as hydrogen bonding, its V-shaped molecules are incessantly forming alliances with each other, the hydrogen ends in the H_2O equation being attracted to whatever oxygen neighbors they might find, forming tetrahedrons.

This Water World, in fact, is like a singles bar gone totally gonzo. The bonds (which in fact explain all of the odd qualities mentioned above) last for the most fleeting of instants—mere picoseconds (a picosecond is one trillionth of a second)—before they've had enough of each other and break up to find other attractors to cling to. On these vanishingly short time scales, water is actually a gel, a hugely complex, restless blob constantly reinventing itself. Within every body of water there is an unimaginably vast amount of activity and change occurring. Always. Non-stop.

And, before the bell rings on our little science class, here's another squirt of water weirdness. From time immemorial, or at least from when the solar system was still forming about 4.6 billion years ago, the Earth has been on the receiving end of a cosmic snowball fight. We are constantly being bombarded by snowballs from outer space—better known as comets—filled with dust, ammonia, dry ice, and an abundance of frozen water.

To be more accurate, we are really just getting in the way, like somebody's pesky little brother. The comets are being lobbed at the sun from the farthest reaches of the solar system, in a place way beyhond the planets that astronomers call Oorts Cloud, and we simply sweep up their debris high in our atmosphere and watch the resulting fireworks. When you see a shooting star, you are witnessing the snowball fight. There's a lot of stuff flying around out there too. Estimates of the amount of meteoric material that hits the atmosphere range from 9,100 to 91,000 kilograms *every day*.

Some scientists believe this is where most of our water came from. So, in essence, Chicken Little was right. The only reason you don't need to duck and run for cover is that most of the cosmic flotsam bombarding us is microscopic.

One eminent physicist, Fred Hoyle, the man who coined the term "Big Bang" (which he intended as a derision—he thought it was a stupid idea), takes a big step even further out there. He argues that space is rife with bacteria, and that comets are infested to the gills. Bacteria brought to this planet by colonized comets, he argues, are the reason there is life on Earth to begin with. This concept, which somebody in the normally repressed science world gave the uncharacteristically sexy name "panspermia," could explain why life began on Earth as early as it did.

If bacteria from space are constantly raining down on us, then it is not so surprising that life—which otherwise seems exceptionally hard to get started—took hold so quickly.

MAYBE HAVING OUR origins as brainless, water-borne germs would explain why we Earthlings are so schizophrenic in our flips between water reverence and water indifference.

Like life itself, the wonder of water isn't something we spend much time pondering over. But we certainly could. It's a humbling substance. When we do stop to think of it, it's easy to slip off into the deep end, to get all profound and unfathomable and feel that ticklish need to spin out Just So stories to give ourselves some sort of psychological anchor against being totally washed away. A very understandable tendency, especially if the one thinking about it is halfway through a long soak in a very relaxing tub of the hot stuff.

I, for one, think the Hindu's story is best.

In the beginning, it goes, there was nothing but a neverending ocean, washing up against nothingness in a pitch-black night filled with a mind-boggling amount of nothing. Well, not exactly nothing. The god Vishnu was there, because he existed before time and creation. And Vishnu's giant cobra, Shesha, was also present, because Vishnu needed something to sleep on. But that was it. Just those two, floating on these peaceful waters until a humming sound came up from the depths. The sound, a great booming "Aum," created energy and light and not only woke Vishnu but set a lotus flower springing up from his navel. In the flower was Vishnu's loyal and wise servant, Brahma. What happens next has several contortions, but Vishnu and the snake end up vanishing, leaving only the god's disembodied voice to order the four-headed Brahma to get to work. So Brahma, the god of creation, divided the divine lotus into three parts to form the heavens, earth and skies. The rest, as they say, is history.

The Inuits' theory has also got a lot of charm to it, though in a very Brothers Grimm sort of way. They pray to the sea goddess, Sedna, for food. There are many variations to Sedna's story too. But she gets screwed in all of them. In one, she grows so large that even her giant parents can't feed her, so her father takes her out in a canoe, dumps her overboard into the icy waters, and then chops off her fingers when she struggles to climb back in. Her fingers become a whale, a walrus, a seal, a salmon—eventually all the creatures of the sea.

Frozen forever, Sedna is the name astronomers have given to the coldest, most distant object yet found in the solar system. Discovered in 2003, she is a red chunk of rock located about eight billion miles away from Earth, well beyond Pluto, out there in the Oort Cloud where all those snowball comets are lurking. If she could, Sedna would probably lob a few Inuit-ward herself.

The classical Greeks called their god of the sea Oceanus, the eldest of the twelve Titans. He was considered to be the origin of all water, and with his wife Tethys created the rivers and streams. His grandson Poseidon (Neptune to the Romans) won the watery realm after defeating his tyrant father, Chronos, Oceanus's son, and the other Titans and then drawing lots with his little brothers Zeus and Hades to determine how to split the spoils. Zeus, of course, got the heavens and the thunderbolts and Hades—lucky Hades—got hell.

In winning the sea, Poseidon was seen as getting a bit of a raw deal. He made the best of things, however. He is said to have had more than one hundred mates. (He wasn't especially particular, it would seem, as they included Medusa, the winged horse Pegasus, a Cyclops, and even Orion, the celestial scorpion hunter.)

The Incas, who, like the Japanese, chose the sun as their primary deity, called their water goddess Yakumama, which translates to Mother Water. In their rivers lives its earthly manifestation—the green anaconda, the world's most massive viper, which is still commonly called Yakumama in Peru.

Gong Gong was what the Chinese called *their* water god, who tried to take the throne of heaven but was beaten out. Being a sore loser, he bashed his head against one of the pillars propping up the skies, resulting in huge floods. Nuwa, a benevolent goddess—or god, depending on which take of her/his life you're indulging in—did her best to patch things up by cutting off a tortoise's legs and propping the pillar up on its back. She also tried to seal the torn sky with stones of seven different colors (creating a rainbow). But the tilt to the northwest was never quite fixed, explaining why the stars slip off in that direction.

Nuwa, herself half-human, half-snake, is credited with creating people from the mud of the Yellow River. But just barely. Her first notion was chickens. Then dogs, sheep, pigs, cows, and horses. It took her seven days to get around to conceiving us.

But Nuwa was just a warmup. The Chinese imagination really got humming when it spun out the Dragon King, or the dreaded Long Wang. (I asked several Chinese-speaking friends to confirm that impressive, if unfortunate, transliteration, by the way.)

Dragons, so the Chinese believe, are associated with water, the east, spring, the color blue and masculine vigor. They have as their great nemesis the giant man-birds called garudas (namesake of the Indonesian national airline) and the phoenix. The latter, which is the guardian of the south, takes red as its color and fire as its element and is, of course, the namesake of the capital of Arizona.

The Celestial Dragon King, one of the four dragon kings, was able to control the clouds and rain and lived in a wondrous, submerged crystal palace guarded by armies of shrimp and crabs.

What's most important for us right now, though, is that the Dragon King lineage stretches directly to Japan. And thus, I like to think, all the way into my tub.

IN THE JAPANESE VERSION of the submerged palace myth, the dragon's abode, built entirely of red and white coral, is located near the island of Okinawa (the word for the submerged palace is *ryugu*, which some scholars have suggested is a perversion of Ryukyu, the chain of islands to which Okinawa belongs).

A story in the *Kojiki*, a collection of folklore completed in 712 A.D., recounts the saga of a hunter god named Yamasachibiko, who, after losing a fish-hook belonging to his brother, the fishing god, makes his way to the palace of the sea god and weds his daughter. Yamasachibiko stays there three years, then, having enlisted all the fish in the sea to help him find the hook, rides home to his brother on the back of a *wani*—which in those days could have meant either a crocodile or a shark.

While he was there, Yamasachibiko and the sea god's daughter, both descendants of the sun goddess, have a child, whose son, Kamuyama-toiwarebiko, is, thank the gods, now better known by the simpler name Jimmu. And, as every Japanese schoolchild knows, Jimmu is the country's first emperor.

Every child also knows the story of Urashima Taro, one of Japan's most oft-told fairy tales, also set in the Dragon King's palace. It's the tale of a common fisherman who saves a tortoise being tormented by a bunch of children. The tortoise turns out to be the Dragon King's daughter, Otohime, and Urashima Taro gladly ends up marrying her (since she has the power to transform herself into a total babe) and spending three wonderful days in the palace. He then gets homesick and convinces the Dragon King to let him return to see his sickly parents, only to find out upon his return to the shore that each day in the underwater world is the equivalent of one hundred human years. His parents and friends have been dead for centuries.

I have always liked this tale. But I have also always wondered what the lesson is supposed to be.

The moral certainly isn't filial piety, since his desire to return to his parents doesn't end very well. It isn't the power of love, either. Before Urashima Taro leaves the undersea palace, the princess gives him a jewelled box as a memento, but tells him never to open it. Lost and lonely in his brave new world on land, Urashima Taro figures the box will somehow help him find his way back to Otohime. So he opens it, suddenly grows old and horribly wrinkled and drops dead on the spot.

EVERY SO OFTEN, I LIKE to make the trip to uptown Tokyo to see the Suiten-gu, a pretty typical little red-and-white shrine with a gray concrete *torii* gate, a roof of curved green tiles, and a subway station right down the street.

As with most established old shrines, the road leading to Suiten-gu is lined with candy stores and souvenir shops. Suiten-gu itself is something of a national franchise of shrines with the same generic label—*suiten* means water god and *gu* means shrine.

Though I like going just for the scenery and maybe to pick up some sweets for the train ride back, Suiten is a sought-after deity. The water god is supposed to grant easy and safe birth, so the place is always crawling with pregnant women clapping their hands in prayer and waving the smoke from a big incense cauldron into their faces or over their bellies. Like most other shrines in Japan, it also has for good measure a couple of tertiary gods on board for people like me who aren't in much need of a pregnancy guardian, but might want to buy a little something to ensure a good rice crop, a passing test score, relief from back pain.

Though belonging to the native Shinto faith, Suiten-gu also pays homage to the Buddhist water goddess, Benten, a lute-playing deity who is the protector of artists, musicians, writers, and fishermen.

Suiten is also another name for the Hindu god Varuna, the many-armed lord of the oceans, the lakes, rivers, and the rains. Varuna, once the supreme god of the universe, has been taken down a few notches over the course of the millennia, but still claims to be omniscient—using the stars to watch the goings-on of the universe—and stands as a divine judge, evidenced by the noose he so often carries.

Though not specifically associated with the bath, the water god shrine—and Shintoism itself—shines a bright light on the Japanese fetish of cleanliness.

In the beginning, the story of their nation goes, there was defilement. "Of old, heaven and earth were not separated," begins the translation of the ancient *Nihongi* chronicles. "They formed a chaotic mass like an egg which was of obscurely defined limits *and contained germs*." (Emphasis added; Hoyle and his panspermia would have been proud.)

The myth goes on to tell of how the gods Izanagi and Izanami created the Japanese islands by sticking their jewelled sword into the primordial brine and letting the muck drip off to form land. It often seems the Japanese have spent the rest of their lives trying to clean up the mess.

Just inside the gates of virtually every Shinto shrine in the country—but almost never at Buddhist temples—stands a place to wash up, usually a large basin made of stone or cement with a few wooden-handled ladles and a towel or two to dry off with. The custom is to douse your hands with the water, then rinse your mouth. Depending on how clean the water looks, the second part can be politely skipped.

Sumo wrestlers do this too. Before each bout, amid their demon-squashing rituals, they spoon out a mouthful of purified water, swish it around between their cheeks a couple times, and then, while holding up a piece of white paper to symbolically hide their actions, deposit it into spitoons at either side of the sacred ring.

With so much dirt out there, Shinto priests have little time for anything other than purification. The idea of cleansing, or *misogi*, is central to the faith. And though it is also carried out with fire, salt, and rice wine, water seems to be the most common cleansing medium.

For the hardcore aesthete, the methods include standing under waterfalls or diving into the freezing ocean at New Year. For rituals, it can just mean a sprinkle here or there.

And at home, it is the bath.

So, I guess, it probably is best not to corrupt your waters.

But, lest a lot of people go broke, enhance away.

xxxii

XI

THE PERFECT SOAK

The mind flows into musings on the great average bathing experience,
the worst shower in the world
and the machinations of advanced toiletry

SO WHAT'S IT ALL about, anyway, really—this whole bathing thing?

To find the ultimate answer to that question, I took another look at that Web site by the Tsumura people, the ones who brought us those ever-popular hot springs essences and have made bathing such a lucrative business.

Their message is unwavering, logical. And in a way, very Japanese. They posit several clear-cut, goal-oriented reasons for bathing. They then state the proper ways to pursue each of these goals, and it's taken for granted that if one observes the correct techniques one can maximize one's bathing benefits.

It's not about anything as frivolous as eating, playing, or sipping a nice hot drink. It's like going on a carefully planned diet. Or taking tennis lessons. Or that tea ceremony we talked about in Chapter One. You don't just do it for fun. You want your black belt.

You want the Perfect Bath.

According to the Tsumura folks, you must approach the bath rationally, like any other science. There is a section that I am particularly fond of that starts with the headline:

"In Japan, main purpose of taking a bath is for relaxation."

It then gives a very detailed, step-by-step explanation of how to properly bathe, written in the style that's used in instructions for installing a fireplace in your home, or for rewiring your kitchen. Here's a typical section:

1. Shoulders should be out of the water. Water level is about 9–10 cm (3.5–3.9 in.) above navel.

2. Water temperature should be tepid. (39–40° C (102–104° F))

3. Stay in the tub about 20 minutes.

And there are even footnotes:

* It will reduce the strain on the heart or the lungs

* It will avoid sharp rise in blood pressure

* By warming the lower part of the body, warmed blood circulates and heats up the entire body without immersing in the hot water.

* Blood needs one minute to circulate the body (between pushed out from the heart and coming back to it). It's difficult to stay in the hot bath more than 5 minutes, and that means blood can only circulate about 5 times in the body. But by taking a tepid bath for more than 20 minutes, blood circulates the body 20 times, and the entire body will be warmed up from inside.

Sure, why not? Makes sense to me. Most of you readers will have noticed by now that I have a bit of a nerdy streak, and I actually find this approach reassuring. It's hardly the final word, though.

As we've seen, I could just as easily pop down to the local rental DVD store and find a very different—and probably more provocative—take on the true essence of bathing in the adult's only section. Or go to the bookstore down the street and get the impression that bathing is really about eating and staying at a nice inn. Or I could track down that water crystal guy and find that it's all about achieving unity with the Greater Wetness.

Or maybe I should just be real quiet and see if my microfauna have anything interesting to say on the subject.

Well, actually, I'd rather not. Despite the Tsumura doctrine, my feeling is that bathing is a pretty fluid concept. I'm not even really sure what my best bath was. Considering how much time and thought I have spent in and on them, it seems that I should.

Since coming to Japan, I have probably taken somewhere between seven thousand and eight thousand baths. And in the course of writing this book, I have had more than my share of significant soaks. Memorable. Educational. Fun. And, yes, relaxing. But I can't name one particular bathing event, or bathing spot, that was head and shoulders above the rest.

Part of that is just personality. I've never been a fan of rankings. But there's a cultural factor here, too. In Japan it's just so easy to get jaded. You tend to get picky. You get spoiled. You can bathe in, or bathe out.

Nevertheless, as Norika the soap girl said, there's just something about having one right there waiting.

I'M THINKING OF A road trip I took to the tiny island of Tane-gashima. Dinner was over. It was still seven o'clock. It was still raining like hell. And I was bored out of my skull.

I did the calculations. I could watch TV for a bit, have a cup of coffee, maybe have a chat with the innkeeper, take a bath—the bath was, in fact, the inn's pride and joy, spacious and rock-lined—and I would still end up in bed by nine.

Having graduated from the sixth grade long ago, that bedtime didn't much appeal to me. The innkeeper was looking at a phonebook and offering helpful suggestions. There was, he said, a big supermarket about fifteen minutes down the road, adding that it was open twenty-four hours a day. He kind of smiled expectantly at that point. I realized that was all he had to offer.

Although there was still a man-size purple pin on the side of the street, the bowling alley right out front had gone out of business a couple of years before and was now a grocery store. And even if I was interested in enlivening my evening by purchasing some carrots or maybe a carton of milk, it was about to close. So that was a no-go. I looked out the window. It was pitch black outside.

I mean no disrespect for the island of Tanegashima. It is famous, after all, for two things. Sometime in 1542 or 1543, a Portuguese trader by the name of Mendez Pinto was taking a walk when he raised his matchlock and blasted a duck in front of local chieftain Tokitaka, who was so impressed by this astounding new weapon that he took shooting lessons and arranged to buy a pair himself, making him the first Japanese to own a gun. Soon guns were all the rage, and Japan would never be the same.

I was there because of Tanegashima's other claim to fame. The island is home to Japan's biggest space center, a sprawling complex of hangars, gantries and launch pads surrounded by the lush, semi-tropical forests and pristine beaches that cover much of Tanegashima's rugged southern tip.

It's a beautiful place. It has, in fact, been described as the world's most beautiful launch site. But Tanegashima was chosen to be the space center precisely because it is so remote and undeveloped that even a rocket launch isn't likely to disturb anything other than perhaps a few scattered fishing boats and a hapless flock or two of birds.

As I sat at the inn, however, all the island's wonders were blanketed in the thick of night. And thanks to the weather, the launch countdown had been put back to T-minus Only God Knows When.

So I was cooling my heels with nothing to write about. Then it dawned on me. I wasn't especially in the mood for one, but I figured that, this still being Japan and all, there had to be a hot springs somewhere. "There's three," the innkeeper said, putting down the phonebook. "Only one would be open this late, and it's on the other side of the island, but it's easy enough to get to."

So that was that. Humble though it was, I now had a plan.

When I got there, the parking lot was nearly full. There were people drinking beer and smoking cigarettes in the lobby. There was laughter. There was a gift shop and convenience store. There was a sushi bar next door, and a small hotel.

This was obviously the place to be; the only oasis of liveliness left on the island after the stroke of eight. And the bath was, well, not too shabby. There was a hot springs, several Jacuzzis, a sauna and the most mind-numbing, spasm-inducing electricity bath I have ever suffered through.

It was clean. It was the real thing—with real minerals in the water, though admittedly in rather diluted quantities. But, hey, whatever. I had a good time. Totally unexpected, too. Which made it all the better.

When I got back to my room that night, I didn't care that it was still raining, that the wind was howling through the trees and that the chances of a launch in the immediate future—and of me getting my ticket out—were somewhere in that twilight zone between slim and fat.

I ended up going there a couple more times before the rocket finally went up and I was free to leave. And I was kind of sorry to go.

I can think of many bathing experiences equally pleasant. But I would still have a hard time ranking these moments on any meaningful kind of scale. Like more days of my life than I would prefer to admit, the baths that were average or disappointing have mostly been forgotten in the blur of time's forward gush. I would even have a hard time recalling my worst bath. It's all down the drain, so to speak.

But in some ways I suppose that's a good thing. There surely have been some ugly ones in there. Unidentified Floating Objects are always a bad sign, and I imagine I've had more than my share of sightings, though to date I have no abductions to report. Cold isn't good either, though at the Super Sento people do pay for the privilege of a freezing dip.

Bad bath experiences are more about people than anything else. People who jump in and start shaving. That's nasty. Or people who bring their own organic bubble machines, if you know what I mean. People who sit too close, are a bit too interested in the scenery, spray their suds all over the place. Those kind of things.

But it's hard to have a really bad bath.

Or is it just me?

NOW THE SHOWER IS a whole other issue.

Showers have a place in the world. They are fast. They are practical, and economical. I grew up with them, like millions or others around the world, and I came out just fine.

But showers don't really do the trick anymore. Not for me, anyway. And I think that is proof that Japan has changed me.

In the introduction to this book, I wrote that the Nagano Olympics was the event that got me interested in hot springs. In an odd coincidence, the worst experience I've ever had while trying to get clean was in a shower at the Winter Olympics in Turin.

I've had better showers in Iraq. In Afghanistan. On a submerged attack submarine somewhere out in the Pacific. Getting hosed off in cold water with a unit of mud-covered Marines after enduring jungle warfare training on the island of Okinawa, when I had two fractured ribs and a welt that started somewhere around my eyebrows and ended just past my toenails— that was far more enjoyable.

Because this experience was so un-Japanese, and because it came in the middle of writing this book—forcing me to think of it with the same scientific and cultural curiosity—I think it's worth a mention. The contrast with what I had come to expect *in the bath* was just so striking.

I'd just put in a long day. A really long day. Twelve hours at a desk, two hours on a bus. It was three o'clock in the morning, and I was looking at a month with no days off, and on most of those days I couldn't even expect a lunch break. I was tired, and I had reason to want a rest.

But I also wanted a bath, and there was none in my room. Instead, there was a shower square. A little, plastic square area, maybe three feet or so on each side, with a raised rim of ankle height in the corner of what I found to be the very ironically named "bathroom." There was a drain in the middle, a shower nozzle, a shower curtain. And that was it.

The soap and shampoo sat on the floor. No dish. The towel rested atop the toilet. No racks. But still, with nowhere else to go, I got in. As the water heated up, I even mused for a moment.

The physics of shower curtains is a fascinating thing. I remembered an article I read in the *New York Times*, entitled "How to Avoid Being Attacked in the Shower." According to the piece, published on July 15, 2001, Dr. David Schmidt, a professor of mechanical engineering at the University of Massachusetts, used $28,000 worth of computer software that he helped develop to simulate the physics of his mother-in-law's bath.

He had apparently been interested in the shower curtain question since he came across it on his doctorate examination at the University of Wisconsin in 1994. The question wasn't completely out of the blue. It was one of those little things about the real world that has long engaged the minds of engineers and physicists, who, like everybody else, do in fact take showers.

Well prepared for the task by his academic training (he specializes in computer simulations of sprays, which is reportedly useful in studying diesel engines), Dr. Schmidt modeled the bath into his program, put in fifty thousand tetrahedral cells to measure movement and pressure and let it rip for thirty seconds at a "bracing blast."

Two weeks and 1.5 trillion calculations later, he had the answer. Well, sort of.

Here's how the *Times* reported his findings:

"The shower's water droplets decelerate under the influence of aerodynamic drag, transferring energy to the bathtub's air, which begins to twist like a miniature hurricane turned on its side. As in the eye of a hurricane, the pressure in the center of this disturbance is low, pulling on the shower curtain. Curtain rods keep the top of the curtain in place, but below the showerhead the bottom of the curtain . . . sucks in."

Got it? Me neither. But it stuck in my mind at the time. Perhaps because the article did close with a helpful suggestion—replace the curtain with a door on your shower.

What some other scientists say is really calling the shots in your shower is static electricity. Their theory works like this: When the water is squeezed out of the shower nozzle with enough force, some of the electrons rubbing against the edges are shaved off of the molecules that are spraying forth. It's like what happens when you rub your arm against a balloon. You're messing with the charges of the two bodies, yours and the balloon's, and the rubbing leaves electrons racing willy-nilly for shelter. That's why when you pull your arm away, your arm hair longs to stick with the balloon. It is attracted to the opposing electrical charge.

Lest you still believe that shower theory is a largely ignored area, let me reassure you. There's more.

We owe this next one to a Romanian engineer by the name of Henri Coanda, who realized that a fluid flowing over a curved surface tends to stick to that surface. The classic experiment to demonstrate this one is a glass held under a faucet. The water from the faucet hits the glass, flows down one side and then clings to it a bit after it hits the bottom, actually flowing back up just a bit before dropping off.

Try it. I did. But, to be honest, after a lot of thought, it seems to me that it is, in the shower milieu, an add on, at best, even though coming up with it was good enough to get Coanda an airport named after him just outside of Bucharest.

By now, however, my moment of musing had passed. I had now moved from theoretical physics to applied psychology.

Aggravation 101.

I started to get pissed off.

I came to the unavoidable conclusion that this curtain possessed an alien intelligence of some sort. The fricking curtain, which was—just as the good doctor warned—attacking me in my fricking Italian shower stall, probably didn't care whether I believed I was in the middle of my own personal hurricane or in a molecular electrical storm—or suffering from Coandan cling.

It was just out to get me.

I had done nothing to deserve this treatment. I had taken the precautions. I made sure that the curtain was on the inside of the little rim, and pulled it snuggly up to both walls so that the water wouldn't go splashing out. But every chance the curtain got, it snuck up from behind me, clinging to my calves, my back, my arms.

The water I so deliberately tried to keep in was now getting all over the floor. The bath mat—yes, there was one of those—was getting soaked.

Because there was no soap dish, I had to bend over to pick the little bar off the floor, and as soon as I did, the curtain *violated* me.

I pulled it off. Maybe a little harder than was really warranted. Okay, I really yanked on it. And it all came plummeting to the floor. I considered myself fortunate that nothing hit me in the head. I also felt kind of good about having shown that damn curtain who's the boss.

But it was a fleeting victory.

I was standing naked, partially covered in soap lather, while the shower sprayed, unhindered, into the drafty room. But I am a good citizen, so I turned off the water and put the curtain and its rail back up again. I finished my shower, and wiped the floor when I got out.

Then I went to bed and, being exhausted, slept.

And the next night, when I returned to my temporary hovel at three in the morning tired and irritable, I fought—and lost—the battle yet again.

I CAN TRACE MY PROGRESS through life in Japan in terms of the type of baths I've had at home.

At first, they were communal.

In college, I had a dorm bath, shared by four people. It was a unit bath. Shower and tub and toilet together in one place, and seemingly cut out of the same piece of tan plastic. There was nowhere to wash off outside the tub, which was deep, in the traditional Japanese style, but which we almost never filled. Showers just made more sense in the tiny space.

When I graduated, I got a real bath. But I still had to share it. My apartment was cramped, in an old, two-story wooden building that was shaped like a U and had a patio in the middle. There were maybe eight rooms. The landlord and his wife lived in the biggest. Down the hall there was a drummer; a struggling architect-to-be and his wife and baby boy lived below me. Across the way were a car salesman and a young woman, the landlord's niece, who worked at a bank.

We were like family. We had barbeques on a little hibachi together in the spring, we took drives in the fall to see the autumn leaves. We hung out in each other's rooms, drinking rice wine and beer.

And we took turns in the bath, which had its own little building, like an outhouse for bathing. It was a concrete block. No frills. In the winter it was freezing and the water took forever to heat up. In the summer it was filled with battalions of exotic flying bugs.

I loved that place.

When it was time to start my own family, I got my first private bath. There was a washing off area outside the tub and a switch in the kitchen to control the heat of the water, which every night was recycled into the washing machine to clean the laundry.

Each bath from there on got more complicated. Each move brought more space. More gimmicks. There were now switches in the kitchen not only to control the water temperature, but to reheat it the next day. While soaking, I could select music from any of a few hundred cable stations to keep me company.

The one bath became a bath and a shower. Then a bath and two showers. But, while bigger and somewhat more convenient, my baths haven't really changed all that much.

Which is very odd, considering what has gone on down the hall.

I HAVE HELD IT IN this long, but I can no longer resist. It's time to take a trip to the Japanese toilet.

While baths have inched forward, in many ways resisting change, toilets in Japan have gone through a true caterpillar-to-butterfly metamorphosis.

When I first came to this country, you squatted. You put your feet on either side, you held your nose and you didn't look down. At regular intervals, the vacuum truck would come around, suck it all up and take it away to God-only-knows-where. Houses in the country still had amulets placed high on shelves over the toilets, and people made offerings to the gods to spare them from the pestilence that, at any moment, could rise up from the depths and wipe out the whole village.

When I came back to Japan for college, my dorm had a Western-style toilet. So I was among the fortunate. But looking back, it was so hopelessly rudimentary. So primitive and unassuming.

It was just a toilet.

Not that I'm really big on complicated toilets. It's just that today even your basic Japanese toilet isn't all that basic. At the very least it's got a heated seat. And it very likely comes with a nozzle to provide a little post-use wash. Many are pressure activated. Wave your hand over a sensor on the wall and the thing will magically flush. In some ladies rooms, there are even noise-making devices to cover up the sounds of all human activity. At homes, there are toilets that analyze your daily contributions and can warn you if you have diabetes or other such ailments.

But while the Japanese toilet is so over the top that it's like something from Batman's cave, the innovations in the bath are much more pragmatic and low-key. Not that there aren't upscale options. The Japanese are very willing to spend good money to have a nice bath in their home, and companies have tried to inspire consumers to put in jets and massage devices and even shockers, à la the commercial electricity bath. But, like fancy imported bath salts, they haven't really caught on.

To me, this is something of a puzzle. Just as the Japanese are taking the toilet to new heights, there are some really futuristic things going on in the bath—elsewhere.

Bathers in the United States, for example, can order something called the Jacuzzi La Scala, a $24,000 "entertainment center" bath set-up that features a flat screen TV and DVD system, and underwater lighting. For a fraction of that, there are steamers and aromatherapy units, or showerheads that mimic an Amazon rainforest or shoot out horizontally. Heated towel racks are a staple of the luxury bath scene, as are all kinds of water-proof TVs, radios, and other sound equipment.

The American-company Ondine, with the motto "Nourish your Soul," introduced the Electric Light Shower, a showerhead with 270 holes in it that emit not only water but a rainbow of colored light from advanced, halogen-powered fiber optics. The shower, which can be purchased in chrome for $2,500 or in 24-carat gold for $15,000, is designed to work under the theory of chromatherapy.

All the really big style innovations going on outside of Japan tend to focus on things like sound and light and entertainment and impressive whirli-gigs—non-water elements that go against the grain of the Japanese bathing mentality.

Watching a movie in a Japanese bath would be dangerous. You'd pass out from dehydration before the final credits. And I'm guessing that many Japanese share this bias; music is really more of a shower thing. You sing in the shower, not in the tub, though most Japanese don't even do that. The one apartment I lived in that had music piped into the bathroom was, in fact, built with foreign tenants in mind.

You can, if you want, find a lot of fancy bath stuff in Japan. But the gizmo focus on the at-home bath front here seems to be latched firmly onto practical issues. Technology has been brought forth to solve the issue of heating and reheating with timers and remote-controlled heaters that you can activate with a phone call from your mobile while on the train home. Scrubbing up afterward is a chore that just about nobody likes, so there are self-cleaning bath tubs. Getting in and out of a deep tub with high sides is a challenge for older people, so designs have been changed—by, for example, sinking the tub into the floor or adding on railing—to accommodate them.

Noritz, a major producer of bathing units in Japan, has taken that several steps further. One bath system is able to determine whether a bather's heart is beating too fast, or, worse, not at all—and to issue an alarm both in the bath and in another room, usually the kitchen. If no movement at all is detected in the bath for a pre-set duration, the system is designed to call emergency telephone numbers that have been entered in its memory. So the graying marketplace, with its very special needs, is already becoming a driving force of future bath design.

But, unlike some of the toilets I've seen here, the technological wonder of a Japanese bath has never really wowed me. Even the various kinds of jets at the Super Sento and the electricity baths are fairly obvious in concept (though the latter is, granted, a very *weird* concept).

Like most Japanese, I still have a fold-up plastic lid with which to cover my own tub, and it keeps the warmth in just fine. I don't have a remote timer, and I don't mind drawing the bath, then working my schedule around how long I can safely assume it will stay warm.

Just give me the basic package—hot, clean water up to my chin—and I'm pretty content.

And I think most Japanese would agree with me on that, too.

SO THERE IT IS. One man's view from the tub. Or actually, a few dozen tubs. And a couple radioactive grottos. And several bug-lined tide pools.

Fittingly enough, as I write these final thoughts, I have just dried off after my nightly bath. I'm still feeling that bubbliness inside, and a comfortable warmth made all the more satisfying by the knowledge that it is an unseasonably cold, spring night outside. The cherries—that other national obsession—are just coming into bloom. I can see them through the window as I sit here with a towel draped around my neck, and a glass of cold apple juice (I save the coffee milk for special occasions) by my side.

Change a detail here or there, and that description probably fits tens of thousands of people in Tokyo at this very moment. To my fellow bathers, I raise my glass. *Kampai*!

A few years from now, I may well have forgotten the details of tonight's bath. Going by the Tsumura guidelines, it wasn't really deep enough. I'm pretty sure it was too hot and I definitely didn't sit still in the water for the full twenty minutes.

So, yet again, I guess I blew my shot at perfection.

But I do feel a little closer to the Greater Wetness.

AFTERWORD

TUB TIPS

Final thoughts on day trips, guidebooks and other practical matters.
Points of particular significance for those who might actually
be thinking of testing out the waters

This book was meant for those who love to read about travel and other cultures. But this final section is particularly written for those who are, in fact, thinking of coming to Japan, or are already here, and may be considering taking a dip or two.

It's about those little things, such as, how likely are you to survive a bath? Where are they? How will you know when to do the full Monty and when to keep it under wraps? Those kinds of things.

There will also be some very subjective recommendations, though I firmly stand by my refusal to claim to know what The World's Best Hot Springs is, or where to find The Best Public Bath in All of Japan.

WHERE ARE THESE PLACES?

Ikaho (Chapter One) and Kusatsu (Chapter Four) are in Gunma Prefecture, an inland province, and take about two to three hours to get to by bus or train from Tokyo. I took the bus to Kusatsu, but I stayed overnight. Ikaho I did in a day, and I felt like I had ample time to wander around and try out the local water.

Shikine Island (Chapter Two) is definitely not a day trip. But it's a great overnighter. And camping isn't the only way to go. There are plenty of little, very reasonable inns for those who would prefer not to be at the mercy of the weather.

Arima (Chapter Three) is also out of the normal day-trip zone for those coming from Tokyo, since it requires a three-hour bullet train ride, followed by an hour or so on the local train.

But the Oedo Onsen Monogatari (Chapter Three) is right smack on the Tokyo waterfront, with a monorail stop just a few minutes' walk away. It doesn't get much more convenient than that.

Yunessun and the rest of Hakone (Chapter Five) is also a pretty easy day trip, though figure on about three hours to get there.

Chapter Six's Otaru, on Hokkaido, is well out of day-trip range from Tokyo, as is the radioactive Misasa (Chapter Seven). But public baths and super-sento (Chapter Three) are all over the capital. Look for one in your neighborhood (but more on that in a minute), or ask a friend for a recommendation/introduction.

Soaplands, a whole world of their own, are also easy to find in the city, just about any city, but go at your own risk. And expect to deal with the usual chicanery of the sex industry—dubious services, false advertising, exorbitant add-on prices. Play it safe, if you play at all, since getting clean may also mean getting sick.

The bottom line is that pretty much wherever you go in this country, you can find a place to bathe. Explore, and see which environment suits you best.

WHERE TO START?

Try the Oedo Onsen Monogatari.

For someone who has never been to a Japanese bath, this place has a lot going for it. It's a bit expensive, but if you're in Tokyo, your total cost will still be much cheaper than traveling outside the city (train fares in Japan being pretty pricey). It can get crowded, but that isn't necessarily bad. For the novice, that means there are lots of people who know what they are doing to observe and imitate, and more people to look at means you'll be less aware of people looking at you. Like Disneyland, the bath house sort of corrals you through, making it easy to figure out. And there are a good variety of baths—outdoors, indoors, fancy, fun. As a bonus, the water qualifies as paleowater, the stuff that the professor in Chapter Two was so interested in. With so many attractions, it's a hot spring/super sento all wrapped up in one.

However, for the more discerning bather, it definitely has its drawbacks. It is big and crassly commercial. And it fails to provide an ambience of natural calm, which was one of the good water doctor's three factors for a healthy bathing experience (Chapter Two). Still, Oedo Onsen Monogatari is an easy introduction to a more traditional hot spring.

Public baths are a bit trickier. As I mentioned in Chapter Three, going to a strange sento can be embarrassing and intimidating—less so, likely, if you can find a relatively big one. In fact, it is probably easier to go to a super sento first, then settle back into your neighborhood bath.

By now all of our bath aficionados are all steamed up; I might as well have suggested that you should always go to McDonalds in a strange town because that way you won't find any surprises on your plate. Yes, it is kind of a cop-out. You may very well have a great experience by dropping in on a totally unfamiliar public bath. That does happen. And it is a wonderful feeling to take that chance and just happen upon a bath that you will remember for the rest of your life.

♨

Then again, it could really suck. And those memories tend to stick also.

GUIDEBOOKS

Don't expect good advice from Japanese bath-focused guidebooks. Honest critiques are still a nascent idea in this country. Instead, they tend to either gush, or be frustratingly just-the-facts. The approach is usually to squeeze in as many baths as were willing to pay or otherwise cooperate in the publishing process, and it seems as though one template is used for just about every guide. On the shelves of my local bookstore, I saw guides that had more than one thousand baths crammed into about 150 pages of magazine. There just isn't much room for creativity or insight.

But the upside is that these guides shine a light on just about any bath you might want to try. And you do get a basic idea of what to expect.

Not many are available in English. But even for those who can't read Japanese, the pictures give a feeling for what's out there. Plus, the format is so rote that it is actually pretty easy to decode the information.

HEALTH ISSUES

No, you can't get any STDs from taking a communal bath.

At least, not that I know of. Well, let's just say I don't know anybody who has.

But there is a tiny element of danger. At the end of 2005, newspapers were buzzing with the death of a family at a popular resort. The family was found in a hollow in the snow. They had apparently suffocated from poisonous gasses emanating from the hot springs nearby.

That was a freak incident. More common, however, are germ-related deaths. As I've mentioned, outbreaks of Legionnaires' disease, in particular, are a problem. Deaths are uncommon, but by no means unheard of.

The danger of getting some sort of infection was probably much higher a few years ago, when both the cavalier attitude of bath owners toward the quality of their water and the sheer number of bathers bringing their microfauna into the baths were at a peak.

A steady flow of hot water through the bath, replacing the old water with fresh water, is crucial, especially when many people are bathing. At the height of the hot spring scandal of 2004 (Chapter One), this became a focus of attention. Many baths that claimed to be properly circulating their waters were in fact simply recycling water that was already used, or not replacing it at all.

Truth is, it's hard to tell if this is being done. Most baths do have a spigot that is quite conspicuously spewing out what appears to be a gusher of fresh water. But looks can deceive. You might not be able to swim in the same river twice, but not so the bath.

However, never fear. Most respectable inns keep clean baths. The probability of getting something other than a good soak is pretty negligible. You're more likely to die on the road getting there.

It is true, on the other hand, that the statistics indicate that heart attacks and strokes are a real concern, although that was all covered in Chapter One. Pregnant women are advised to be careful, and many baths are too hot for children. For the most part, the risks are avoidable if you bathe responsibly; talk to your doctor if you have concerns.

The worst side effect I ever experienced after bathing was sore eyes. After a couple of days bathing in Kusatsu, which is famous for the acidity of its waters, my eyes burned whenever I closed them. It made sleeping difficult for a night or two.

I've had a bit of dizziness after staying in a hot bath for too long. And I've stunk for a while after getting in an especially smelly one. Shikine Island's natural essence (Chapter Two) had me stinking of sulfur for days.

THE TOWEL THING

Now, how to operate those little towels.

You can get them very cheaply at just about any bath—the perfect souvenir. For some, they are collectibles. A friend of mine who runs a company that does geological surveys for hot spring resorts makes a point of bringing his own towels from exotic baths on his various outings. It's kind of like having a lot of stamps on your passport, or stickers on your luggage.

I have mixed feelings about them, however. After all, where do you put them?

The first place seems pretty obvious. From changing room to bathing area, they are used to casually prevent full frontal nudity, not that there won't be a good deal of that anyway in the course of bathing. For men, the towel is generally held in one hand in front (but not usually on) one's private parts. The more nonchalantly this is done, the better. Otherwise, you're just drawing attention to yourself.

Now, this use of the towel I fully support. Seems quite sensible to me, since, as we saw in Chapter Six, a lot of in-your-face nudity can get pretty overwhelming. The towels may not really cover much, but the courtesy of putting them out there is, in my opinion, very social-minded.

The towels may or may not be used in the washing-off process. A little rub a dub on the back, that sort of thing, then—once the towel has been very carefully cleansed of any residual suds—it goes out front again for the walk from washing zone to bath.

If you're in a mixed bath, that's probably where the towel should stay. Women years ago began using larger towels that can be wrapped around the torso to cover both top and bottom.

Such encounters are, however, pretty rare. Usually you'll be in there with members (no pun intended) of your own gender.

And here's where I tend to diverge from bathing orthodoxy. The general thinking is that they belong on the top of your head, folded up into a little square, like an apprentice model's composure book. But I've always thought that looked really stupid. I mean, let's be honest. Nobody looks good with a towel sitting atop their head. It just doesn't work.

Women are not expected to do the towel-on-the-head thing. Probably because they accept that it looks ridiculous. I envy them that.

You do want to have one, though.

They are convenient in the pre-bath wash-off, and they're useful for wiping the sweat off your face while soaking. There's also that psychological factor. Having a little towel with you makes you feel less naked and exposed, even if it is just in your hand or placed on the side of the bath. Bathers very often will hold the towels over themselves as they move from the washing area to the bath itself.

I do that myself. Then I drape mine around my neck or put it aside until I need to wipe my face. No one has ever complained, or looked at me funny, so I guess there is some leeway on this issue.

But be sure of one thing. If you use the towel to wash off with, get all the soap out of it before you take it to the bath. The spread of soap film from a dirty towel is on par with the spread of radiation from a nuclear attack.

MR. MANNERS

Here's an obvious one.

Don't be a jerk. Seriously. Don't swim around. Don't splash. Don't squirt people. Don't fart.

I was in a bath recently with a man from Poland, a good guy I might add, who insisted on falling backward into the water, repeatedly. He had a grand time splashing a couple of Chinese bathers who were too polite to tell him to knock it off. He howled like a wolf and shouted cat calls at the women on the other side of the bamboo partition.

Okay, he was drunk. And he was happy. But that shouldn't be everybody else's concern. It is interesting how often people who aren't used to bathing publicly act this way. Perhaps it's something to do with trying to mask the embarrassment of being naked in front of others. Or the opposite—the thrill of letting it all hang out is just too much to control.

But, even in the bath, it's best to keep some of it in.

A corollary to that: If you go to a crowded public bath, there is a high likelihood that you will get splashed. And not necessarily by a jerk.

It just happens. There often isn't a whole lot of space. And when you are showering, sitting there on your stool, whistling your favorite song and moving the shower nozzle around to wash yourself off, the spray tends to go all over the place. It happens even if you are being conscientious and trying to keep your runoff water to yourself.

Some people seem utterly unconcerned by this. It still bugs me. But in the scheme of things it's pretty minor.

NAKED ENCOUNTERS

Know when to strip. Wearing a swimsuit when everybody else is totally nude is as offensive as popping out totally naked in a swimsuit zone.

Usually it's pretty obvious which is which. In public bathhouses, you bathe naked. I can't think of any exceptions. In mixed areas at the newer theme park–style baths, swimsuits are often the rule. There will almost certainly be signs. There will also almost certainly be other people around to provide some guidance.

Rustic hot springs can be a bit more challenging. Places like the outdoor bath in the monkey reserve that I mentioned in Chapter Five aren't uncommon. Often they are empty too, leaving you on your own to figure out what is kosher.

Be judicious. That tempting hot spring near a crowded train station may well be in plain view of all the people on the platform—maybe not a good idea to strip down and hop in. Then again, there are times when it is okay.

The issue is even more complicated when both sexes are involved. It is increasingly common for baths to contain a mix of naked men and swimsuit-clad women. Again, these are more often than not baths that are way out in the country somewhere, clearly exposed to whoever might be wandering around nearby. Strictly speaking, everybody should probably be naked (or everyone should be swimsuited). But in the interest of being inclusive, the rules are usually bent in favor of female modesty.

I have mixed feelings about this, too. While I can understand the modesty stuff, being naked around bathers who aren't only draws attention to your own nakedness. It becomes more of an issue, not less. So I usually avoid baths where I think this might be the case. I guess it's what psychologists might call reverse modesty.

Or maybe it's just my twisted sense of equality. At any rate, the trend definitely is toward women wearing swimsuits into the baths whenever there might be a mixed crowd, while for men, the little towel remains the most common denominator.

SOAPING DOWN

Unless you are really in the boonies, the bath will have a washing off area. Use it—at least to rinse off before you get in.

Most baths will have shampoo and soap, a bucket, and a stool to sit on. Sometimes it's just a shower head, or just a faucet and the bucket. In the countryside, it may just be a bucket. If that's all you've got, then douse yourself with water from the bath itself.

There is probably something of the spit-in-the-ocean factor involved here. It might not really make all that much difference from the hygienic perspective. But it makes a world of psychological difference to the other people in the bath.

It's gross to see somebody just hop right into the bath with you without washing off first. Especially their, well, you know. It makes you want to hop right out.

I have been in baths with people who not only didn't wash off first, they actually began shaving once they got in. Barbarians. And these were Japanese people, who should have known better.

Also, get all the suds off before you move on to the bath itself. Coming in all sudsy is worse than not washing off first at all.

A MORE PHILOSOPHICAL QUESTION

While pretty much everyone agrees on washing off first, many connoisseurs believe that it is best not to wash off afterward. The thinking is that you don't want to wash off all the good minerals and whatnot that you have just gone to the trouble of immersing yourself in.

I can see that. And since you are already out, and thus no longer a concern to anybody else, why not?

I wash off before and after. I suppose I just am not all that determined to suck the medicinal wonder out of every last mineral I come in contact with. And I'm also kind of concerned about the other whatnots that are coming out of the bath with me. Then there is the smell factor. Many hot springs baths are pretty pungent. Like I've said, I smelled for days after my trips to Kusatsu and Shikine Island. And that was after some serious scrubbing.

CHATTING IT UP

Japan is a little like a library sometimes. People just don't strike up conversations with strangers all that much. Even with people you know, conversations in public places such as trains, where not everyone has someone to talk to, are expected to be hushed.

Schoolgirls are somehow exempt from this fundamental social rule. They can be as loud as they want to be. Go, girls.

But I've found that the bath is something of a gray zone. I have had some good conversations with hitherto strangers in baths, mostly in outdoor hot springs where things are just naturally more relaxed and open. Really hot baths, on the other hand, discourage chatting simply because the heat is so all-encompassing.

If you want to start up a conversation with someone, be low-key about it. Avoid topics like your skin condition or your conversation partner's physical attributes, good or bad. Comments on the bath itself are usually a safe starter.

Also, be aware that when there is an international element added in, a whole new dynamic starts up. There is a stereotype among the Japanese that foreigners, pretty much all non-Asian foreigners, are gregarious and talkative. So if you are a non-Asian foreigner, some Japanese may assume you'll enjoy a chat with them. On the flip side, if you initiate a chat, you will likely be fulfilling your newfound Japanese friend's stereotype.

When you live with it for a long time, the invasion of a stereotype like this into the routines of life can be kind of annoying. But it can also be with a nice ice-breaker.

Call it a toss-up.

COFFEE-MILK

When you get out of the bath, if you see some of that coffee-milk that comes in thick little glass bottles, try it.

It's great. It's really refreshing. And I'm not being paid to say this.

It's not just a personal thing, either. Fresh coffee-milk, an old-style Japanese mix that is very sweet and rich, and very unlike the latte you might get at Starbucks, is sold at a large percentage of baths, both public bathhouses and hot springs. So there must be a lot of people out there who share my opinion.

I don't know what it is. But there is something about it that works wonders to quench a thirst and restore a bit of energy after a good, hot soak. Much better than, say, a beer, which, while pleasantly cold, just doesn't have the same restorative powers.

Consider making coffee-milk part of your bathing experience.

ON THE CHEAP

It is possible to make hot springs bathing an indulgence you can afford to do more than once a year. One of the best ways is to skip the inns—or skip the sleepover.

All good resort towns have plenty of places to bathe that don't require overnighting at an expensive hotel or inn—which is what really sends the cost of hot springing through the roof. Often, there is only a token fee in the several-hundred yen range.

Such baths are usually run by the town and are open to the general public. All of the resorts mentioned in this book have such facilities, and some of them are excellent. The baths described in the chapters on Ikaho and Shikine were all either free or dirt-cheap. The bath in Arima set me back just a few-hundred yen. Most of the hot springs that I have visited over the years fall into this category.

If bathing is really your main concern, and you're not traveling too far to make it back the same day, hit the public facilities. They are clean, the water isn't messed with too much, and the price can't be beat.

You can also try paying the somewhat larger fee to use the baths at the inns. For around ¥1,000 or so, it is fairly easy to find an inn that will allow you to bathe without staying the night.

A FEW MORE WORDS ABOUT SEX

Despite all the pornographic fantasies out there, hot springs aren't really a venue for the randy. They are just too damn hot for sex or any other strenuous physical activity.

I'm talking about sex in the bath. Inside the bath. Public bathhouses are pretty much beyond the scope of this discussion, since the bandai is watching all the bathing. Nothing is going to happen there—as evidenced by the ubiquitous sento pornography, which is almost always limited to a variation on the Peeping Tom theme.

The growing number of private baths at hot springs—baths that are, for example, on the veranda of private rooms, or baths that are rented out for private use, often by the hour—are becoming something like a surrogate for what the Japanese quaintly call "love hotels."

But, even with privacy assured, the heat of the baths still has a way of cooling things off. Repeated soaks in hot springs are very taxing physically. So, my humble suggestion to all the lovers out there: If you are going to indulge in both, it's best to focus on one, and enjoy the other in moderation.

And get a room.

xxxiv

ILLUSTRATIONS

i. A classic home bath, circa 1950. Note the wooden stool for washing, the wooden bucket upside down on the wooden lid that rests atop the wooden tub used to keep the heat in the water as long as possible. Even the walls and the floor are wood. Like kryptonite to Superman, mold is the great nemesis of the traditional Japanese bath, however, and great care must be taken to combat it. Today, these wooden baths are a vanishing breed, highly prized and very expensive. The best material is *hinoki*, or Japanese cypress, which adds a very natural scent to the experience.

ii. A popular solution to sanitary problems is tiles, of course, as shown in this 1970s era home bath. The tub is plastic, though metal is just as impervious to mold. By putting the tub flush against the wall and leaving virtually no space between it and the floor, the designer has also kept the cleaner in mind. Also note the heating (and re-heating) unit alongside the tub. It is basically the same as the unit my host family bought for me thirty years ago, except that one came with a shower.

iii. The main street in Ikaho is actually this flight of stairs that lead from near the train station up to the Shinto shrine at the top of the hill, where the source of all the village's good fortune gushes forth—a fountainhead and outdoor bath. Cars must snake their way around side streets. *Photograph courtesy of the Ikaho Onsen Kanko Kyokai.*

iv. The sea-level view from the deck of the Tokai Kisen ship out of Tokyo bound for the island of Shikine. On fair days it is a beautiful journey, with the blues of the sky and water, and the greens of the lush forests on the passing islands. Flying fish and intrepid seabirds dart in and out of the waves. But as a reminder of from whence it all came, a plume of white steam and gas coming from the island of Miyake is often visible.

♨

v. The first hot springs I stumbled upon on Shikine was the nicest. Despite its outdoor coastal location, it had little changing rooms for men and women, little yellow buckets and faucets to wash off. The baths were lined with patches of colorful flowers. It was almost enough to make you forget about the sea lice and the film of brown muck from the iron sulfides in the water.

vi. Yes, that's me. And, no, I'm not naked. Swim trunks are pretty much the rule on Shikine, though I was alone most of the time. The next bath was just a short hike down a tree-lined path and a very nice, white-sand beach was only a ten-minute walk in the opposite direction. Once I changed into my trunks here, I spent the rest of the day in them, dipping through three hot baths and then chilling in the frigid ocean.

vii. We Love the Bath! Everybody is happy in the steam! Or so say the kids in this poster put out by the Tokyo public bath association. But wait. Are those two little boys with suds all over their hands actually standing *inside* the bath? My God, call the police! *Poster courtesy of the Tokyo Sento Association.*

viii. This traditional public bath has all the classic elements, from the high chimney out back to the temple-inspired sweep of the roof. The curtain over the door says *yu*, which means hot water. The rehydration station (soda machine) and the man going in all dressed in his never-been-in-or-out-of-fashion clothes could both be just as easily out of 1960-something as they could have been circa last week. *Photograph by Shinobu Machida.*

ix. Lockers in a traditional sento. The best public baths have a real timelessness about them, and this photo could have been taken in 1960 or, perhaps, in 1860. These cubbyholes for your belongings aren't for shoes, by the way. You probably took those off and put them in a locker by the door. Or you may have just left them in the entranceway, just as you would if you were going into a friend's house. *Photograph by Shinobu Machida.*

x. If you've been in a public bath in Japan, you've seen this mural—or at least a variation of it. Mount Fuji is the undisputed king of the bath wall. So majestic. So cliché. But I'm not complaining. Note the low wall dividing the men's and women's areas, but leaving the space feeling connected and open. Usually the two sides are virtually identical, but many public baths alternate the sides, just for variety. *Photograph by Shinobu Machida.*

xi. Mt. Fuji isn't the only art subject to be found in public baths. The tiles in the bathing area come in different levels of lavishness, though there are only a few artists who specialize in tile painting still working today. Fish are common, and carp are especially favored because they are considered auspicious and the symbol of strength and hardiness. Scenes of nature are more often seen on the men's side; the tiles on the women's side are often scenes from traditional folk tales meant to entertain the children. *Photograph by Shinobu Machida.*

xii.   Another promotional poster put out by the Tokyo *sento* people, this one by renowned artist Tadanori Yokoo. *Poster courtesy of the Tokyo Sento Association.*

xiii.   This is about as typical a photo of an outdoor bath, or *rotenburo,* as you are likely to see anywhere. And no, those ladies aren't really naked, either. They are covered by full torso towels. (It is truly an art how those towels can be hidden in bath advertising.) Ironically, in real life, these three probably would be naked. They are on the women-only side of the Oedo Onsen Monogatari bath, and thus need not cover themselves so cautiously. *Photograph courtesy of Oedo Onsen Monogatari.*

xiv.   Ah, the good old days, as represented by one section of the Oedo Onsen Monogatari. The idea here is to make the experience go far beyond the bath, by creating the atmosphere of a samurai era festival. The stand in the right-hand corner sells hot noodles, and other stalls feature other dishes and traditional entertainment. I assure you that all of these comfortable-looking people are secretly worrying about the sudden opening of their *yukata* robes. Well, maybe some of them are. Well . . . I would be. *Photograph courtesy of Oedo Onsen Monogatari.*

xv.   In this print by the celebrated woodblock artist Utagawa Hiroshige (1797–1858), a bath attendant rushes to help a bather who has discovered that things can go wrong with a *Goemonburo,* one of the baths named after an unlucky thief (page __). With the fire directly underneath the bath, problems do occur, as one can imagine. *Photograph courtesy of Kanagawa Prefectural Museum.*

xvi.   A feast for the eyes—one small part of the dinner courses at Kusatsu's Hotel Ichii. Dainty and delicate. And sometimes even delicious. Multiply several times and you may be getting close to the desert course. Dining is so intrinsic a part of the bathing experience for most tourists that photos of the food are often given more space in glossy guidebooks than those of the baths themselves. *Photograph courtesy of Hotel Ichii.*

xvii.   Whacking the waters. Though it has been reduced to a display for the tourists, replete with old ladies singing and dancing on a stage in the background, this stirring ritual was once used to cool the hot spring waters so that bathers could get in without scalding themselves. *Photograph courtesy of the Kusatsu Onsen Kanko Kyokai.*

xviii.   Gushing spigots of water are a common sight in hot springs villages. Many are used as foot baths, with strollers taking of their shoes and socks and sitting for a brief soak before heading back out on their way. Others often have ladles for anyone wanting a drink. Beware—the best mineral water isn't necessarily the best tasting. **Photograph courtesy of the**

xix. Erwin von Baeltz probably did more than any foreigner to bring Japan's bathing fetish to the world, and to start shaping it into the science that it has now become. He even packaged his own bath-inspired concoction of healing waters. *Photograph courtesy of the Kusatsu Onsen Kanko Kyokai.*

xx. A Edo-period ranking of Japan's baths done up in the style of sumo-ranking programs. At the top of the list are the champions, and not surprisingly—given that it was written by a Kusatsu native—the town is one of them. Today it adorns a wall of the Kusatsu hot springs museum. *Courtesy of the Kusatsu Onsen Kanko Kyokai.*

xxi. The 2004 promotional poster for Tokyo public baths. Artwork by Tadanori Yokoo. *Poster Courtesy of the Tokyo Sento Association.*

xxii. A sketch of a Shimoda public bath house by William Heine, a German-born artist who accompanied Commodore Perry's expedition. The sketch, more imaginative than literal, still shocked the American public when it was published in a narrative of the trip, and it was subsequently removed from later editions.

xxiii. The bandai at a public bath house. Note how his raised seat gives him a good vantage point, and yet doesn't put him in a position of simply gaping at the customers. *Photograph by Shinobu Machida.*

xxiv. This one is pretty self-explanatory. In more than two decades living in Japan, I've only come across a few of these, and all were at discos or bars. When this one went up in front of a bath house on the northern island of Hokkaido, things got very hot, indeed. *Photograph courtesy of David Aldwinckle.*

xxv. The entrance to Ryokan Ohashi, an inn in Misasa. Along with the delights of radio-active bathing, the inn had a very relaxing atmosphere. Like at most Japanese inns, along with greeting your arrival and bidding you farewell, attendants also lay out your bedding and set up your dinner table right in your room.

xxvi. One of the baths at the Misasa inn where I stayed. This one isn't radioactive. Just hot and very refreshing. Note that although the bath is indoors, it offers a terrific view of the nature outside. This is a hallmark of hot springs in Japan. In the gully just beyond the bath flows the Miroku river.

xxvii. Every pack of smokes should have a little uranium in it, don't you think? After all, if you're going to suck poisonous materials into your lungs, you might as well add a little radioactivity. Actually, the NICO card adds on a tiny, tiny amount of action. But you don't need to tell your friends that. It would ruin the fun. *Photograph courtesy of Oak Ridge Associated Universities.*

xxviii. A street view of the brothels in the Yoshiwara district, circa 1880. By this time, prostitution at public baths had been banned, and the yuna—or "hot water girls"—were forced to move here to continue their business. Though unidentified, it is very likely that today this street is lined with Soaplands—the brothels' contemporary cousin. *Photograph by either Kozaburo Tamamura or Ogawa Kazumasa; Boyd/Izakura Collection.*

xxix. There weren't any fancy tiles in Norika's room, but this photo of a typical Soapland room gives you the basic idea of the setup. Note the tub and the big metallic-hued air mattress. In Norika's room, there was also be a big stool, the kind she slid under once she got all lubed up. *Photograph by Shinobu Machida.*

xxx. The 2003 promotional poster for Tokyo public baths. Artwork by Tadanori Yokoo *Poster Courtesy of the Tokyo Sento Association.*

xxxi. Just a few of the dozens of bath additives on the shelves of my local drug store. Most mimic the contents of natural hot springs. The middle shelf alone offers the essences of about two dozen of Japan's most famous spas.

xxxii. Water for bathing is run from the individual taps lining the bath wall or scooped from the bath using an *oke*, or bucket. Traditionally made of wood, they come in all colors of plastic today. Some people use their personal bucket as a carry-all to bring their bathing items—hand towels, shampoo, etc.—to the public bath.

xxxiii. Like the buckets, regulars at the public baths often eschew the provided soaps and other amenities for their personal choice of items. Some baths, such as this one, offer space for them to leave these on the premises. *Photograph by Shinobu Machida.*

xxxiv. A bath scene captured by an unknown photographer, circa 1880. Even though she's on the receiving end of what looks like a good scrubbing, the young girl looks quite soothed by the experience. *Boyd/Izakura Collection.*

ACKNOWLEDGMENTS

I have found over the years that writing is, essentially, a solitary endeavor. After all the reporting and the interviewing and the experiencing is over, the real task begins. You must hide yourself away, alone, and get to work. But, at the risk of sounding schizophrenic, I never felt that way while writing this book. Alone I was, but I had my muse sitting on my shoulder as I wrote, guiding me through each chapter, inspiring me on to the end.

So, here's to my muse. May we work together again very soon.

But another thing I have learned over the years is that any work worth doing involves the help of other people. And in getting *Getting Wet* done, I certainly had my share of guides and advisors.

My gratitude goes to editor Greg Starr, who steered me straight and patiently waited as I went off to Kashmir and Kabul and Seoul and Torino, tossing our writing schedules out the window each time.

Also, for her helpful comments and gentle editing touch, my appreciation to Tiffany Watson. And to Shoko Imai, who helped track down many of the photos that appear in these pages.

Passage into Soapland was an endeavor that would not have been the same without the help of Kozo Abe, who freely contributed his time and considerable researching talents, and to Chisato Kakinuma, who provided not only invaluable introductions but expert insight.

This book involved dozens of interviews, both in and out of the bath, and for all those who so graciously agreed to indulge me in my many questions I am greatly indebted.

Finally, I must thank my daughter, Sara, for introducing me to the watery words of Keats, and my son, Eugene, for letting me use the computer.

（英文版）ニッポンお風呂紀行
Getting Wet

2006 年 6 月 26 日　第 1 刷発行

著　者　　エリック・タルマジ

発行者　　富田 充

発行所　　講談社インターナショナル株式会社
　　　　　〒112-8652　東京都文京区音羽 1-17-14
　　　　　電話　03-3944-6493（編集部）
　　　　　　　　03-3944-6492（マーケティング部・業務部）
　　　　　ホームページ　www.kodansha-intl.com

印刷・製本所　　大日本印刷株式会社